MONSTERS
IN THE NIGHT

MONSTERS IN THE NIGHT

LISA REGAN

📖 SCHOLASTIC

www.scholastic.com

This edition published by Scholastic Inc., 557 Broadway, New York, NY
10012 by arrangement with Amber Books Ltd.

Scholastic Canada Ltd.
Markham, Ontario

Scholastic Australia Pty. Ltd
Gosford NSW

Scholastic New Zealand Ltd.
Greenmount, Auckland

Scholastic UK
Coventry, Warwickshire

1 2 3 4 5 6 7 8 9 10

ISBN: 978-0-545-26351-1

Editorial and design by
Amber Books Ltd
Bradley's Close
74-77 White Lion Street
London N1 9PF
United Kingdom
www.amberbooks.co.uk

Project Editor: Sarah Uttridge
Design: Keren Harragan

Printed in Shenzen, China

Picture credits:
All main artworks © IMP AB except p13, 16, 36, 50, 52, 62, 72, 89, 90 by
International Book Management, www.ibm.gb.com © Amber Books Ltd.
All small artworks by International Book Management, www.ibm.gb.com
© Amber books Ltd. All backgrounds by Keren Harragan and Rick Fawcett.

CONTENTS

INTRODUCTION

Do you know what's lurking in the darkness? Can you sense the rustle of something that's alive out there in the undergrowth? Did you hear the muffled squeak, or the crack of a twig, that gives an unmistakable clue?

Don't get too scared! Many creatures hunt and eat in the nighttime, making them nocturnal, but they're not all man-killers. Many of the animals contained within this book are completely harmless to humans. Some of them, such as the koala and the binturong, live their lives in the trees, munching peacefully on leaves or fruit. Others shy away from any sort of human contact so they rarely harm people, even though they are venomous or have killer claws and teeth.

Of course, some animals will attack if they feel threatened. The hippo is one of Africa's most dangerous animals, even though it doesn't actually kill to eat meat. Its size and its temperament mean it must be treated with the greatest respect and due caution. And although it feeds at night, it is alert enough in the daytime to show up occasionally and scare the tourists on safari.

There are certain creatures lurking within these pages that can be a real threat to humans. They have savage claws and vicious

Gray Wolf

teeth for slashing and biting, or needlelike stingers for delivering deadly venom. And you'll find the ultimate nighttime nightmare creature: an animal with razorlike teeth that are so sharp they don't even wake their victim when they pierce the skin, such as the Vampire Bat. Clearly, nocturnal hunters are a force to be reckoned with—or avoided at all costs!

So, who's frightening and who isn't? Each creature, from the shyest to the scariest, has been assessed for its fear factor, which you can find out using the "Level of Threat to Humans" gauge. This will help you decide whether you're ready to venture outdoors after dark. This rating takes into account all sorts of factors, including whether the animal could put you into the hospital, if you would need a special antidote for its venom, or the BIG ONE: probability of death.

Scary stuff!

Barn Owl

DEATH'S HEAD HAWKMOTH

WINGS
This is one of the fastest moths. It has long, narrow wings and a streamlined body to help it fly quickly.

TONGUE
A hawkmoth has a tongue like a coiled spring, called its proboscis. It uncurls to feed on honey and tree sap. Other types of moth have a longer proboscis to reach into flowers for nectar.

THORAX
The death's head hawkmoth gets its name from the distinctive skull markings on its back.

COLORS
Bright colors and markings such as the yellow stripes on its abdomen help to keep away predators.

The death's head hawkmoth not only looks striking, it has unusual features, too. It can squeak loudly if it is handled or annoyed. Instead of sucking nectar from plants, as most moths do, these moths steal honey from beehives. They raid the hives and can move around without being stung by copying the scent or the noise of the bees, as a form of disguise. They are among the fastest-flying insects, and can reach speeds of more than 30 mph (50 kph). In ancient times, the moths were often linked to war or death.

HOW BIG IS IT?

AT A GLANCE

Lifespan:	2–3 months
Weight:	0.2 ounces (7 g)
Wingspan:	Up to 5 inches (13 cm)

World Habitat
The three species of death's head hawkmoth live in Europe, Africa, and Asia. They migrate long distances in order to breed.

Endangered Status — Not Listed

DID YOU KNOW?

• The moth is featured in horror stories and movies, probably because of its spine-chilling skull markings and name. In Bram Stoker's novel *Dracula* the vampire sends the moths to a lunatic named Renfield, to eat, and the poster for the movie *Silence of the Lambs* shows the main character with the moth over her mouth.

• There are three species of death's head hawkmoth. Each of them is in the genus *Acherontia* (from the Greek river *Acheron*, which the ancient Greeks believed was linked to the underworld) and has an additional part to its name that is linked with death.

• The caterpillars are huge, growing to 6 inches (15 cm) long. Their favorite food is potatoes, so they are often seen on agricultural land.

• It used to be known as the "bee robber" for obvious reasons.

Low **High**
LEVEL OF THREAT TO HUMANS?

The death's head hawkmoth hatches from an egg as a caterpillar. The caterpillars are known as horn-worms because they have a spine on the end of their tail. The caterpillars are bright yellow with purple stripes, and use their mandibles (mouthparts) to bite if threatened. They eat constantly until they reach their pupal stage, and emerge from their cocoon as an adult.

EAGLE OWL

SIZE
This powerful predator is one of the world's largest owls, and weighs up to 7 pounds (around 3 kg)—the same as an average human baby.

"EAR" TUFTS
These feathers are sometimes called horns, and do not help the owl's hearing at all. They stand upright on a male and droop down on a female.

PLUMAGE
The bird's mottled brown feathers and pale belly help to camouflage the owl in the daytime.

EYES
An eagle owl has unusual, and very striking, bright orange eyes. It can see well in the daytime, and can stare straight at the Sun. This is *extremely* dangerous for humans because looking straight at the Sun can cause people to go blind.

These huge owls have a wingspan of around 6 feet (1.8 m)—the height of a fully grown man. Their size means they can hunt and kill large prey such as herons and deer, although they are quite happy to fill up on rats, squirrels, and hares. They nest in rocky crevices lined with a few feathers, choosing places on cliff ledges, in caves, and even quarries, where they can watch for approaching danger. They perch motionless until night falls, when their fantastic sense of sight and hearing enables them to find food.

HOW BIG IS IT?

AT A GLANCE

Lifespan:	20 years
Weight:	7 pounds (3 kg)
Length:	23–30 inches (58 76 cm)
Wingspan:	58–80 inches (140–200 cm)

World Habitat
Eagle owls are "Old World" owls, found across Europe and much of Asia but not in the Americas.

Endangered Status   Least Concern

DID YOU KNOW?

● Their call sounds more like a single "Wooooo" than the "Twit twoo" sound suggested for storybook owls.

● One pair of breeding eagle owls in the north of England became infamous for attacking people walking their dogs. Most (maybe all) eagle owls in Britain are thought to have escaped from captivity.

● The Finnish soccer team is nicknamed after the eagle owl ever since one flew onto the field during a game in 2007 and watched for a few minutes from the crossbar of the goal!

● Eagle owls and other horned owls belong to a different group from barn owls. Horned owls are known as "typical" owls; there are more types of typical owl than barn owl.

Low   High
LEVEL OF THREAT TO HUMANS?

An eagle owl's striking features are its size, its eyes, and its ear tufts. These may be for camouflage—to break up the owl's outline in the daytime and make them harder to see—or to attract a mate and to help recognize individual birds or species. Less obvious are its amazing talons, which are bigger than a leopard's claws. Eagle owls have been seen fast asleep but still clutching their dinner!

TAIL
A firefly's tail contains chemicals that glow and produce a luminous green light, which the firefly can flash on and off.

WINGS
Despite their name, fireflies are beetles, not flies. Like all beetles, they have wings (although some females are wingless and look more like the larvae).

FAMILIES
Fireflies are all members of the Lampyridae family and are closely related to the Phengodidae family of glowworms.

LIGHT
Making light is known as "bioluminescence." Fireflies do it to attract a mate, but it may also warn predators that they taste really bad.

Fireflies are also known as lightning bugs, and can be seen flashing away in the nighttime. They give off light to attract other fireflies to help defend their territory or warn off predators. Often, the males fly around and flash to attract the females. Each species has its own pattern of flashes, so a female of the same species will flash back to signal to a male. Some species live in trees, where the females wait to find a mate, while others have aquatic larvae with gills. Fireflies are usually found near rivers, streams, ponds, and lakes.

HOW BIG IS IT?

AT A GLANCE

Lifespan:	About 2 months
Weight:	Less than 1 ounce (20 g)
Length:	0.2–1.5 inches (0.5–3.8 cm)

World Habitat
Fireflies live on all continents except Antarctica. They are found in warm, humid areas in temperate and tropical forests, in marshes, and fields.

Endangered Status   Not Listed

DID YOU KNOW?

• Although each species has its own flash, some sneaky species copy the flash of other species to trick them into coming closer. Then they eat them!

• Scientists marvel at the efficiency of a firefly's flash. A lightbulb gives off heat energy as well as light energy—as much as 90 percent of energy is lost as heat. A firefly's glow is 100 percent light energy.

• Fireflies are not good food. When they are attacked, they give off drops of blood that taste awful and can be venomous. Many animals have learned not to eat fireflies.

• Scientists have found many uses for the chemicals fireflies use to glow. These include detectors on spacecraft looking for life in outer space, and medical studies into cell diseases such as cancer.

Low   High
LEVEL OF THREAT TO HUMANS?

Firefly larvae are predators, and eat dead animals, earthworms, and other invertebrates. They follow the slime trails left by snails or slugs, and sometimes gang up to attack larger creatures. Their front end has a sickle-shaped mandible, which the firefly uses to inject venom into prey to paralyze it. When they become adults, many fireflies feed on nectar and pollen, but some may eat nothing for their short lifespan!

FLYING SQUIRREL

WINGS

A flying squirrel's "wings" are actually a furry flap of skin on each side of its body, spreading from its wrists to its ankles. The flap is called a patagium.

TAIL

The tail is not used for steering as is often thought—it is too flat for that. It is used for balance when gliding and climbing, and for slowing down in flight.

WHISKERS

The squirrel uses the sensitive hairs on its snout to help find its way in the dark. It seems that squirrels often navigate through thick trees with their eyes closed!

EYES

Like so many nocturnal creatures, the flying squirrel has exceptionally large eyes to collect as much available light as possible.

There are several different types of flying squirrel in the world. Two of them are New World creatures, the northern and southern flying (seen here) squirrels. Both are about the size of a tree squirrel, but differ in one very obvious way: they have wings! They cannot truly fly like a bat, but they are extremely good at launching themselves from trees and gliding down to a chosen spot, often up to 165 feet (50 m) away. Asian flying squirrels are much bigger and can travel as much as 1,300 feet (400 m) from branch to branch.

HOW BIG IS IT?

DID YOU KNOW?

• To escape from the grasp of a predator, a flying squirrel has a special feature, known as a "breakaway" tail. The surprised predator is left holding a portion of fur but no squirrel!

• A flying squirrel's whiskers are the longest of all squirrels, for its body size.

• Like all rodents, squirrels can regurgitate but cannot vomit!

• The giant flying squirrel of Asia has such a large patagium that it looks as if it is wearing a cloak! This makes walking difficult, so it has to clamber along the branches in a clumsy, waddling way.

• Some American flying squirrels eat truffles (a fungus that grows below ground), which are a delicacy worth hundreds of dollars.

Low   High
LEVEL OF THREAT TO HUMANS?

Unlike most squirrels, flying squirrels come out to feed at night. By day they stay safely away from predators, hidden in holes in tree trunks. Their favorite foods are nuts, berries, buds, shoots, leaves, and even eggs and baby birds. The squirrel stands high on a branch, decides where to land, sways a little, and then launches itself and glides smoothly to another tree or branch lower down.

MOSQUITO

WINGS
Like other members of the order Diptera (true flies), mosquitoes have two wings and two wing stubs that help them balance.

LEGS
Their six jointed legs are very long. Each ends in a foot with sticky pads and tiny hooked claws, which enable them to walk up walls and across the ceiling.

MOUTH
The mouth parts are called the proboscis. Females have a long proboscis, which they use to pierce the skin of their victim and feed on the blood.

BODY
The rear part of an insect's body is its abdomen. A malarial mosquito's abdomen has a pointed tip, and you can see the blood inside as it feeds.

Mosquitoes are the world's most dangerous creatures, in terms of the deaths they cause to humans (and livestock). The malarial mosquito is just one type. As well as carrying malaria, which kills at least one million people each year, these bugs also carry elephantitis and encephalitis. Different types of mosquito also spread yellow fever and other fatal diseases. Their mouthparts are like a syringe that punctures the skin and sucks out blood, and also injects a substance to stop the blood from clotting, which makes you itch if you are bitten.

HOW BIG IS IT?

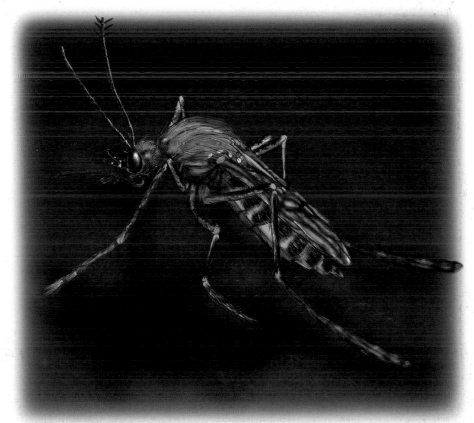

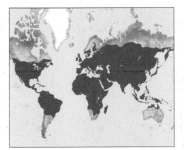
DID YOU KNOW?

• The name mosquito means "little fly." There are at least 2,500 species of mosquito around the world. Malarial mosquitoes rest on a surface with their head pointing downward. Other mosquitoes sit parallel (flat) to the surface.

• The female mosquito keeps sucking blood until its abdomen feels full. If the nerve that senses this were to be cut, scientists think she would keep on drinking until she burst.

• The life cycle of a mosquito, from egg to adult, can last from one week to several weeks. The eggs grow in water—anything from a swimming pool or lake to a dirty puddle.

• Only female mosquitoes bite. The males have a short proboscis and feed on the nectar of plants. Females drink nectar, too, but need blood for their eggs.

Low   High

LEVEL OF THREAT TO HUMANS?

The mosquito is rarely active in the daytime, but comes out to cause havoc as darkness falls. They make an annoying, whining hum as they fly around, and can sense body odor, temperature, and breathed-out air to track down their victims. Male mosquitoes have bushy antennae for hearing things, which are tuned in to the exact frequency of the buzzing of females of their own species.

PIPISTRELLE BAT

The pipistrelle bat is tiny. It is the smallest bat found in Britain, and also the most common. It can squeeze through a space less than 1 inch (2.5 cm) wide. They spend their days roosting in buildings, trees, rock crevices, and specially built bat boxes, then come out by their hundreds as night falls. They hunt in the air, catching small insects such as gnats and moths. One pipistrelle bat can eat 3,000 gnats per night! It uses echolocation to "see" in the dark. This enables it to find prey and avoid bumping into things during flight.

HOW BIG IS IT?

EARS
A pipistrelle bat has spikes of flesh in its ears to receive the echoes that bounce back from solid objects.

WINGS
Its wings are smaller than the height of this page, but are strong enough to propel the bat quickly, changing direction in a flash. The bats fly about 16–32 feet (5–10 m) above the ground.

SIZE
A pipistrelle weighs only up to one third of an ounce (8 g) and is small enough to sit easily on the fingertip of an adult human.

ARMS
Like all bats, pipistrelles have modified arms that support their wing membrane. Their finger bones are extremely long and stretch the skin to enable the bat to fly.

AT A GLANCE

Lifespan:	Up to 16 years
Weight:	0.1–0.3 ounces (3–8 g)
Length:	1.5 inches (3–5 cm)
Wingspan:	7.5–10 inches (19–25 cm)

World Habitat
Pipistrelles are found on farms, woodlands, and wetlands across Europe and into Asia, Africa, and the Middle East.

Endangered Status   Least Concern

DID YOU KNOW?

• Bats emit calls and they listen to the echoes of their calls to judge distances and to identify objects. This is known as echolocation.

• The eastern pipistrelle is a type of bat found in very small numbers in parts of the United States. Another species, the soprano pipistrelle, can be told apart from the common pipistrelle only by the frequency of the sound it makes.

• A pipistrelle mother has only one baby at a time, usually in June, which can fly when it is about three weeks old. Twins are much more common for bats in central Europe. The babies are called pups.

• Pipistrelles generally eat as they fly, but if they catch a large moth they will find somewhere to perch as they eat it.

Low   High
LEVEL OF THREAT TO HUMANS?

During the winter, the pipistrelle hibernates to avoid the harshest weather conditions. Sometimes thousands of bats hibernate together in a cave or building. The bats hang upside down, gripping with their feet, and their body slows down to save energy. When the weather warms up, the bat wakes up and flies off in search of food again. One cave in Romania was found to contain 100,000 hibernating pipistrelles!

VAMPIRE BAT

LEGS
Vampire bats hunt on the ground so they have adapted strong back legs to enable them to walk, run, and hop toward their prey.

TEETH
Sharp side teeth are used to shave off a patch of fur and a thin layer of skin, and then the razorlike front teeth bite through the flesh to draw blood.

TONGUE
A vampire bat does not actually suck blood, but uses its tongue to lap it up, like a cat drinking milk.

WINGS
Bats are the only mammals that can truly fly—some other mammals can glide on outstretched flaps of skin. Bats flap their wings but use their wing claw for climbing up a tree in order to take off.

The three species of vampire bat are true night hunters. Hundreds of them roost in caves, mines, hollow trees, and old buildings during the daytime, keeping safe from predators. After dark, they emerge from their hiding place and fly off in search of a warm-blooded victim such as a sleeping farm animal, tapir, bird, or even a human. Usually, the bat lands nearby and approaches on the ground. Infrared heat sensors in the bat's nose help it to find a good spot where blood flows close to the surface of the victim's skin.

HOW BIG IS IT?

AT A GLANCE

Lifespan:	Up to 9 years
Weight:	0.5–18 ounces (14–50 g)
Length:	Up to 3.5 inches (9 cm), head & body
Wingspan:	8 inches (20 cm)

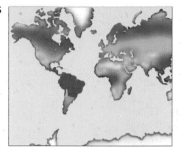

World Habitat
Vampire bats are found in Central and South America, in dry places or humid areas.

Endangered Status   Least Concern

DID YOU KNOW?

• Vampire bats might look strange when they walk, but are actually good runners, reaching speeds of up to 5 mph (8 km/h).

• The bat injects its saliva, which contains an anesthetic, into the wound to stop the victim from feeling anything. An anticoagulant in the saliva helps the blood ooze without clotting.

• Vampire bats do not kill their victims by drinking their blood, but they can spread disease. However, the anticoagulants in their blood are of great interest for scientists and medical research.

• Vampires feature in famous horror stories such as *Dracula*, *Twilight*, and *True Blood*. Like vampire bats, they feed on blood, but they prey mostly on humans, biting their neck and often killing their victim.

Low   High
LEVEL OF THREAT TO HUMANS?

Feeding lasts for up to 30 minutes. Vampire bats can lap up around 1 fluid ounce (25 ml) of blood—almost two tablespoons! Young bats often go hungry if they wake up their victim by accident. These bloodthirsty creatures need to feed every two or three days, or they will starve. Unusually, a hungry bat can beg for food from another vampire bat, which will regurgitate some of its own meal and share it.

COCKROACH

The cockroach has got a bad reputation as a filthy pest, but around 99 percent of them are actually useful for scavenging garbage. The cockroach often picks up diseases on its feet, though, which can be spread onto food that people eat, which makes them sick. It hides under tree bark, stones, logs, or in caves during the day and comes out at night to eat. Its enemies include birds, mammals, other insects, and a tiny parasitic mite that lives on the cockroach and feeds on its body.

HOW BIG IS IT?

BODY
A cockroach's flat, oval body is perfectly designed to squeeze through tiny gaps to find food or to escape from danger.

SPIRACLES
Cockroaches (and many other insects) have small holes called spiracles for breathing. They do not need to breathe through their mouth.

ANTENNAE
The antennae are used to find food and moisture. They are long and very sensitive to track down the tiniest amounts of sustenance.

LEGS
Sensors on the legs, and at the roach's rear end, are used to detect tiny air movements, which warn the cockroach of danger and enable them to scuttle to safety.

AT A GLANCE

Lifespan:	Up to 22 months
Weight:	0.02 ounces (0.6 g)
Length:	2–3 inches long (5–7.5 cm); 1 inch (2.5 cm) wide

World Habitat
Cockroaches live in almost every part of the world that is inhabited by humans.

Endangered Status   Not Listed

DID YOU KNOW?

● The Madagascan hissing cockroach has about 40 young (called nymphs) at one time. Each baby is about the size of a small watermelon seed.

● A cockroach can survive without its head! It will die only after about a week, because it can't drink anything.

● The cockroach's body is protected by a hard outer shell called the exoskeleton. As it grows, it gets rid of its old shell and reveals a new, larger shell underneath. Often, it will eat the old shell to get back the nutrients in it.

● Unlike mosquitoes, cockroaches do not carry diseases by biting. They do wander around dirty, germ-ridden areas, though, and may transfer the germs to human homes, leading to their reputation as pests.

Low   High
LEVEL OF THREAT TO HUMANS?

Cockroaches have been on earth at least 300 million years—that's longer than any other winged insect. There are around 3,500 species of cockroach. The Madagascan hissing cockroach is unusual because it has no wings, and it can force air out of its breathing tubes to make the noise that gives it its name. They usually move slowly but if they are disturbed they hiss and then run off quickly.

DUNG BEETLE

BODY
The dung beetle is a type of scarab beetle, with a fat, oval-shaped body and a hard shell. Some are shiny and jewel-colored but are often brown or black.

MOUTH
The beetle uses its specially designed mouthparts to extract moisture and nutrients from the manure of animals such as camels, elephants, and cattle.

LEGS
Dung beetles have strong front legs for digging and for fighting other dung beetles when finding a mate. They use their long back legs for rolling the dung balls.

ANTENNAE
Scarabs have different antennae from other beetles, with clubs on the end that spread out into finger or leaf shapes.

WINGS
A beetle's wings are hidden beneath hard wing covers.

Without the humble dung beetle, the world would be a dirtier, smellier place, with a lot more poop lying around! Dung beetles specialize in cleaning up animal waste and carrying it off to make use of it. Some of them eat the dung themselves, while others lay their eggs in it. The eggs hatch into larvae, which have chewing mouthparts to munch away at their poopy surroundings. After pupating, the larvae emerge as adults. Dung beetles are unusually good parents (as far as insects go). They stay with their young grubs for two months.

HOW BIG IS IT?

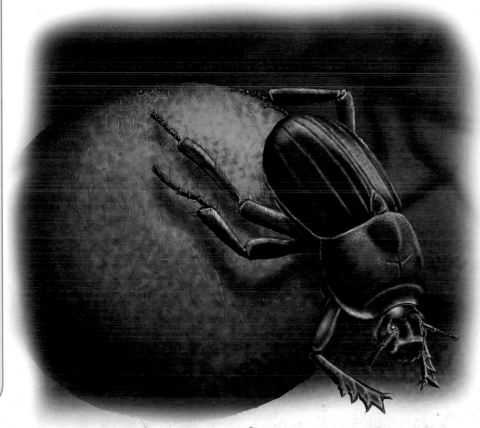

AT A GLANCE

Lifespan:	18 months
Weight:	1.2–3.2 ounces
(empty)	(35–80 g)
(full)	6.4 ounces
	(160 g)
Length:	0.04 inch
	(1 mm)–2.25
	inches (6 cm)

World Habitat
Dung beetles live all around the world except the very coldest places.

Endangered Status   Not Listed

DID YOU KNOW?

• Scarab beetles were worshiped by ancient peoples, including the Egyptians and the Shamans. To the Egyptians they symbolized the heavens and the underworld because the beetles could both fly and dig. Some shamans used beetles in fortune-telling rituals.

• The super-strong male horned dung beetle can pull more than 1,000 times its own weight—that's the same as a human pulling six double-decker buses! Most dung beetles can roll a ball of manure that weighs 50 times more than they do, and can bury 250 times its own weight in a single night's activity.

• As well as eating dung, the beetles also eat other dung beetles and their eggs.

• One heap of elephant dung weighing 3 pounds 5 ounces (1.5 kg) can have up to 16,000 dung beetles in it.

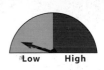

Low   High

LEVEL OF THREAT TO HUMANS?

Dung beetles may be tunnelers, rollers, or dwellers. This means that some of them dig into the dung, some of them roll balls of the stuff, and some of them just live in piles of it. They have a great sense of smell, which enables them to track down far-flung dung and roll it up to take it away (sometimes over long distances) to a place where it can be buried.

RED-KNEED TARANTULA

FANGS
Under attack, a tarantula will display its fangs. Most spiders close their fangs together sideways, like pincers, but tarantulas strike downward to puncture the skin of their victim.

EYES
Red-kneed tarantulas have eight eyes around their head, but their eyesight is not that good. Instead, they use sensitive hairs on their legs to feel their way around.

LEGS
The front two legs are used for holding food. Their other six legs are used for walking. They have palps on the ends, which help them smell and taste.

BODY
A spider's body is split into two parts, the abdomen (at the back) and cephalothorax (the front, or "head").

Most tarantulas use several weapons for attack (and defense). Their fangs are used to stab their victim and inject poison. This kills the creature and dissolves its insides into a mushy liquid, which the tarantula sucks up like a milkshake. Their legs and body are covered with bristly, barbed hairs that the spider can flick at enemies. These hairs irritate the areas they touch, and can be dangerous around the eyes and mouth. Their venom is not serious for humans but is enough to kill prey larger than the tarantula, such as frogs, lizards, birds, bats, and small snakes.

HOW BIG IS IT?

AT A GLANCE

Lifespan:	Up to 30 years
Weight:	2 ounces (57 g)
Length:	Legspan up to 11 inches (28 cm); body: 3–4 inches (7.5–10 cm)

World Habitat
The red-kneed tarantula lives in scrubland and desert in Mexico and Central America, but is becoming rare.

Endangered Status — Near Threatened

DID YOU KNOW?

● Tarantulas don't build webs to catch their food, but sneak up on their prey and pounce on it, more like a cat. The red-kneed tarantula digs a burrow in the ground to live in, and lines it with silk.

● After a large meal, a tarantula can go for a month without eating.

● Tarantulas are nocturnal and rely on touch more than eyesight.

● Tarantulas are getting rarer as they become more popular as pets and are removed from the wild. Their main natural enemy is a kind of wasp that stings the tarantula and lays its eggs in the paralyzed body. The eggs hatch and the wasp larvae eat the tarantula alive.

● A tarantula can grow back a leg if one is lost.

Low   High
LEVEL OF THREAT TO HUMANS?

Some types of tarantula have made friends with the dotted humming frog, and they help each other out. In return for protection from snakes and other frog-eaters (including the tarantulas themselves), the frogs live in the tarantula's burrow and eat the ants that prey on the spider eggs. Both creatures are nocturnal, and the frogs have been seen sitting between the spider's legs at the mouth of its home.

THICK-TAILED SCORPION

TAIL
A scorpion's tail is split into sections that enable it to bend right over its back. It has a venomous stinger at the end.

PINCERS
The thick-tailed scorpion's pedipalps, or pincers, are smaller than in many scorpions because their venom works so fast they don't need to pin down their prey.

LEGS
Scorpions are arachnids, like spiders, and so have eight legs on the front part of their body (called the cephalothorax).

BODY
Arachnids have two body parts: the cephalothorax and the abdomen (which contains the internal organs). Their body is covered with a flexible but tough outer skeleton (exoskeleton).

Thick-tailed scorpions, members of the Buthidae family, are extremely venomous. They are active at night and often find their prey by touch, or wait in hiding until a tasty creature comes past. Some of these types of scorpion can spray their venom up to 3 feet (1 m) if they are angry or under threat. Their venom is highly dangerous, but few humans are stung because the scorpions live away from people, although they sometimes live in thatched roofs. They have fine hairs on their body and legs to feel their way in the dark.

HOW BIG IS IT?

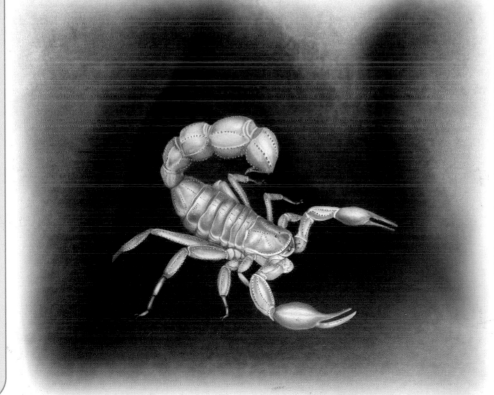

AT A GLANCE

Lifespan:	3–5 years
Weight	0.9 ounces (25 g)
Length:	1.5–5.5 inches (4–14 cm), most at least 2.75 in (7 cm)

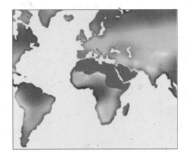

World Habitat
They are found throughout the dry regions of the Middle East and Africa.

Endangered Status   Not Listed

DID YOU KNOW?

• Scorpions are the most ancient group of arachnids, dating back more than 350 million years—before the dinosaurs first appeared.

• Generally, larger scorpions are less venomous than smaller ones—but the thick-tailed members of this family are an exception to this rule.

• These scorpions are kept as pets, but do not like being handled. As well as spraying a mist of venom, which can be dangerous if it gets in your eyes, they can sting in different directions by moving their tail from side to side as well as forward and backward.

• Scientific studies have found that young scorpions are more likely to use their stingers than older scorpions, which have probably learned to conserve venom.

Low   High
LEVEL OF THREAT TO HUMANS?

These scorpions spend their daytime in burrows made under rocks or dug into the sandy ground. Their top tail sections have a rough surface. Scraping their stinger along this surface makes a distinctive hissing sound. A scorpion has two eyes on top of its head, and more pairs of eyes along the front. Female scorpions give birth to live young, which ride on their mother's back.

WELS CATFISH

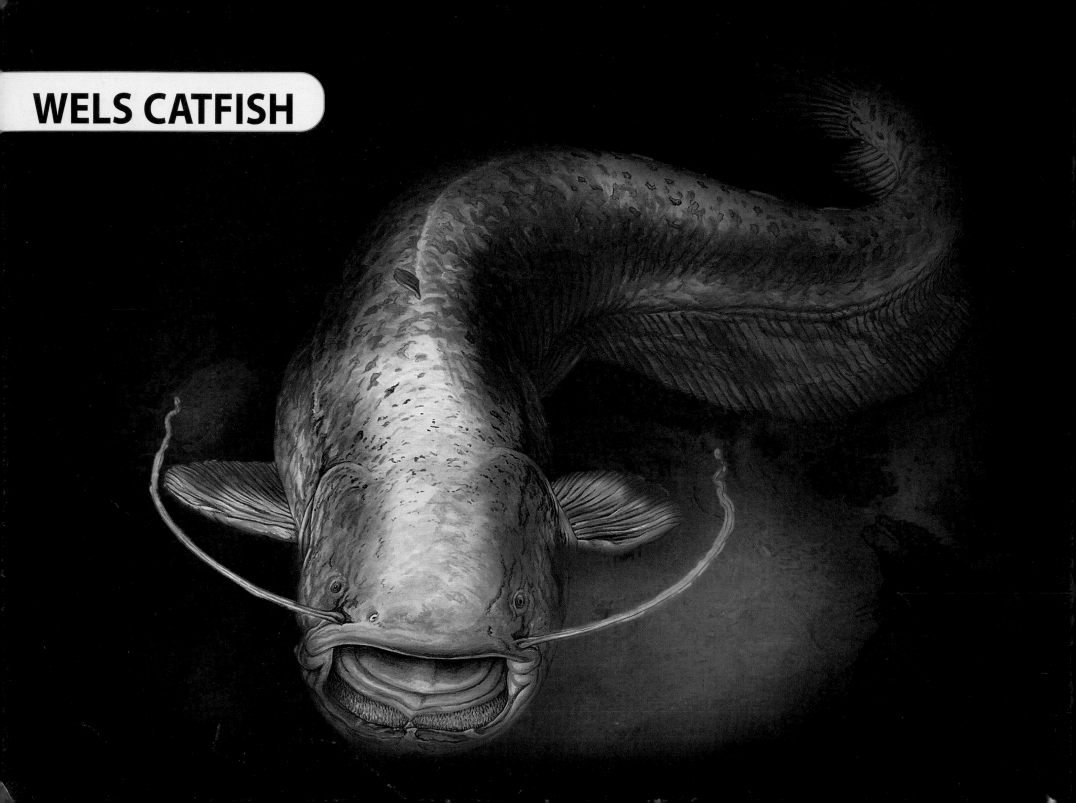

The wels catfish is one of the largest, and certainly the longest, freshwater fish in the world. It grows too big to eat (although smaller ones are edible), and its eggs are poisonous to humans. An average adult wels catfish can weigh as much as a child, and the heaviest ones weigh as much as two grownups. It uses its barbels to feel its way in the darkness of night or in murky water, and can gulp down worms, fish, and water bugs. Bigger wels catfish also swallow frogs, water rats, snakes, and ducks.

HOW BIG IS IT?

BARBELS
The whiskery parts around a catfish's mouth are called barbels, and are probably what gives a catfish its name.

BODY
The wels catfish has a very long, tapered body with a wide, flat head—a lot like a giant tadpole. It has no scales, so is slippery like an eel.

JAWS
The catfish's wide mouth is lined with rows and rows of hundreds of tiny little teeth. These make the inside of its mouth as rough as sandpaper.

FINS
The catfish uses its pectoral fins, which are located near its head, to stir up the water and confuse potential prey before sucking it into its cavernous mouth.

AT A GLANCE

Lifespan:	Up to 40 years
Weight:	110–661 pounds (50–300 kg)
Length:	Up to 10 feet (3 m), average size 5 feet (1.5 m)

World Habitat
The catfish lurks in the waters of lakes and slow-flowing rivers across Europe, including the inland Baltic and Caspian Seas.

Endangered Status — Least Concern

DID YOU KNOW?

- The official world record for the size of a wels catfish is 202 pounds (91.6 kg) but unofficially, people have caught specimens weighing up to 330 pounds (150 kg).

- For centuries, people have told tales about man-eating wels catfish. In 2008 there was a string of attacks in Lake Schlachtensee, outside of Berlin, Germany, which people said were a wels catfish.

- Some wels catfish have been caught with human remains in their stomach. Experts think the fish came across bodies of people who had already drowned—and took advantage!

- In the breeding season, a male catfish builds an underwater nest where the female lays a large number of eggs—more than 10,000 eggs for every pound of her body weight! The male stays with the eggs until they hatch.

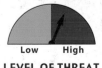

Low   High

LEVEL OF THREAT TO HUMANS?

During the daytime, wels catfish lurk in quiet, dark places such as among thick water weeds and hollows under the riverbank. Their dark, greenish-black body is well camouflaged. In hot, thundery weather it might hunt in the daytime in a feeding frenzy. Its teeth are razor-sharp and used to scrape its prey like a cheese grater. Its strong body and enormous size make it difficult for fishermen to catch.

ANGLERFISH

ALLURING LURE
The strange piece attached to the female anglerfish's head is a "lure," which she uses like bait on a fishing hook, to attract prey right to her mouth.

MOUTH
An anglerfish's mouth is shaped like a crescent moon, and is packed with sharp, see-through teeth.

SIZE
Anglerfish come in all sizes. The biggest are up to 3 feet 3 inches (1 m) long. Most are much smaller, however, measuring less than 1 foot (30 cm).

FINS
Some anglerfish have pectoral (side) fins like arms, which they use for walking around on the floor of the ocean.

There are around 200 species of anglerfish and, it's fair to say, most of them are ugly. Many live in the deepest parts of the ocean, where there is little or no light. Sometimes, to attract prey, they can make their long lure glow in a process called bioluminescence. Often, the anglerfish stays still in the water or half-buried in the sand and simply waits for some unsuspecting prey to swim within reach. The anglerfish can eat food bigger than its own body because its jaws open extra wide, and its stomach stretches.

HOW BIG IS IT?

AT A GLANCE

Lifespan:	May be up to 100 years
Weight:	110 pounds (50 kg)
Length:	8–40 inches (20–100 cm)

World Habitat
Most anglerfish live deep in the Atlantic and Arctic oceans, although some live in shallower, warmer waters.

Endangered Status   Not Listed

DID YOU KNOW?

• An anglerfish's teeth slope backward and stop anything it eats from trying to swim out to safety.

• The deep sea anglerfish is round, like a basketball, and nicknamed "the black devil" because it looks so scary. It lives more than 3,000 feet (915 m) down in the ocean where it is cold and totally dark.

• Most anglerfish are poor swimmers; they either "wobble" through the water or stay in one place and wait for food to come to them.

• In Japan, the meat of the anglerfish is considered a delicacy, and said to taste like lobster.

• Bioluminescence creates a bluish-green light a little like that given off by a firefly (see pages 12–13). It is created by bacteria living on the lure (called esca).

Low   High
LEVEL OF THREAT TO HUMANS?

One of the most unusual things about the anglerfish is the way they mate. It's hard to find each other in the vast ocean depths, so once a male meets a female, he latches on to her body and stays there—forever. His body gradually disappears, starting with his digestive system as he no longer eats, and then his brain, heart, eyes, and most of his body just fades away.

BAT-EARED FOX

EARS
Its most striking feature, the fox's ears are at least 5 inches (12 cm) long and super-sensitive to even the smallest sounds.

FACE
Anything would look small in comparison to those ears, but the fox's muzzle is only little, with a short, narrow mouth.

TEETH
A bat-eared fox has more teeth than any other non-marsupial mammal. It has 48, including up to eight extra molars at the back of its mouth.

COLOR
The fur is a sandy-gray color, which helps camouflage the fox. Its belly is lighter in color and its feet, tail, and tips of its ears are dark. They have a raccoonlike mask around their eyes.

This small African fox certainly stands out in a crowd! As well as its huge ears, its teeth and its diet make it different from other members of the dog family (canids). Instead of feeding on meat from other mammals, the bat-eared fox mainly eats insects. It hunts at night, listening for the tiny noises of rustling creepy crawlies, and licks up termites, crunches on grasshoppers and millipedes, and even takes on scorpions and spiders. That's why it has shorter canine teeth (to tear flesh) and more molars (for crushing and grinding hard foods).

HOW BIG IS IT?

AT A GLANCE

Lifespan:	Up to 10 years
Weight:	6.6–11 pounds (3–5 kg)
Length:	18–26 inches (46–66 cm),
Tail Length:	9–13½ inches (23–34 cm)

World Habitat
This fox lives mainly in parts of eastern and southern Africa, but some live in Namibia, Botswana, and Zimbabwe.

Endangered Status   Least Concern

DID YOU KNOW?

● Bat-eared foxes mate for life, which means one male (called a dog) and one female (a vixen) have babies and stay together as partners. They both rear the cubs, or kits, together.

● They do not suffer as much as some creatures during the dry season, as long as they can find food. Much of the moisture they need comes from the body fluids of the insects they eat.

● These little foxes are fast and nimble, and can often outrun or outmaneuver predators, dodging away from the snapping jaws of a hyena or jackal.

● Bat-eared foxes make their homes on African grasslands called savannas. They live underground in burrows, often ones that they have borrowed from a meerkat colony.

Low   High
LEVEL OF THREAT TO HUMANS?

The fox's huge ears can detect tiny noises in the dark, to help it track down food and avoid stealth attacks from predators such as lions, jackals, and cheetahs. The shape of its ears also help it to keep cool in its desert home because the large surface area contains lots of blood vessels, which allow extra heat to escape. Although they hunt in the dark, they often play and sunbathe in the afternoon sunshine.

FANGS
The snake has a pair of fangs that swing down from the roof of its mouth, ready to stab venom into its prey.

HEAD
A pair of heat-sensitive pits between the snake's eyes and nostrils enable it to find objects that are warmer than their surroundings. This enables the snake to hunt in the dark.

COLOR
The copperhead has a reddish-brown body with striking pale and dark bands or stripes.

EYES
The eyes of a copperhead have vertical, slit-shaped pupils, a bit like a cat's eyes in bright light. Nonpoisonous snakes that look similar to the copperhead have round pupils, like a human.

The copperhead is a highly venomous type of viper that kills and eats mice, frogs, birds, spiders, and insects. It does bite humans but its venom isn't strong enough to kill a healthy person, and they bite in self-defense only. Their mouth has rows of fangs lined up behind their main fangs, ready to replace the ones being used. In summer, they are totally nocturnal, and can hunt in complete darkness detecting prey by using special heat-sensitive pits on their head. At other times, they like to sunbathe on the ground or in trees.

HOW BIG IS IT?

AT A GLANCE

Lifespan: 18 years
Adult Weight: Undetermined
Adult Length: 24–47 inches
                (61–120 cm)

World Habitat
Copperheads are the most widespread venomous snakes in the southeastern United States, but are rarely found in the west or north.

Endangered Status   Least Concern

DID YOU KNOW?

- A copperhead has fangs up to one-third of an inch (7.5 mm) long. The bigger the snake is, the longer its fangs are. Newborns have fangs that can inject venom just as powerful as an adult's venom.

- Many copperheads are killed on the roads because they freeze if they are in danger. If you find one, stay well away from it and it will leave you alone.

- Baby copperheads have a yellow tail, which is thought to act as a lure to get prey to come close enough to catch.

- If a copperhead gets angry, it vibrates its tail really quickly. It releases a smell from its rear end to make it unappetizing to predators. Some describe the smell as being like the smell of cucumbers, while others say it smells more like cat urine!

Low   High
LEVEL OF THREAT TO HUMANS?

When a copperhead has its mouth closed, its long fangs swing backward to the roof of its mouth. When it opens its mouth to strike, the fangs swing forward and the snake sinks them into its prey to inject strong venom. It keeps hold of smaller creatures until they die, but the snake will track larger prey until the poison takes effect.

GROUND PANGOLIN

SENSES
Pangolins have no visible, external ears but they do have very good hearing. Their eyesight is poor, but they have a good sense of smell.

SNOUT
They have no teeth, but have an extremely long tongue to collect ants and termites. After the pangolin swallows the food, its stomach muscles "chew" it.

CLAWS
A pangolin has long, curved claws to help it pull open termite mounds. The claws are so long the pangolin has to walk with its feet turned inward.

SCALES
The pangolin is covered with scales made from keratin (the same as your fingernails, or a hedgehog's spikes). These sturdy scales protect the pangolin's body and make up about one-fifth of its total body weight.

The ground pangolin has the longest tongue of the eight species of pangolin. It can reach up to 16 inches (40 cm) away to catch ants and termites. When not in use, the pangolin curls its tongue curls back into a storage space in its throat and chest area. Pangolins swallow stones or sand to help grind up food inside their stomach. The ground pangolin hunts at night. When it finds a nest, it tears it apart with its strong claws.

HOW BIG IS IT?

AT A GLANCE

Lifespan	20 years
Weight:	33–40 pounds (15–18 kg)
Length:	20–23⅓ inches (40–50 cm)
Tail Length:	16–20 inches (40–50 cm)

World Habitat
Ground pangolins are found only in the woodlands and savannas of eastern and southern Africa.

Endangered Status   Least Concern

DID YOU KNOW?

- Saliva makes the pangolin's tongue sticky. The pangolin pokes its tongue into a nest and wiggles it around to collect lots of insects, and then pulls it into its mouth to swallow.

- Pangolins are good at swimming and often live near water.

- A mother pangolin gives birth to one baby at a time. At birth, the baby has soft, pale scales, which start to harden within a few days.

- The baby rides on the mother's tail unless it is threatened, when it slides underneath her and is protected when she rolls into a ball.

- The pangolin has to protect itself against angry ants and termites as it eats. It closes its nostrils, keeps its eyelids tightly shut, and presses its scales close together to stop insects from crawling through to its skin.

Low   High
LEVEL OF THREAT TO HUMANS?

The main predators of the ground pangolin are leopards, hyenas, and humans. For protection, the pangolin rolls into a ball, covering its softer underside and head so that only its hard scales show. These scales have very sharp edges that can injure an attacker, and can be moved in a cutting action on anything that is poked between them. The pangolin can give off a strong smell, too, like a skunk.

HIPPOPOTAMUS

MOUTH
A hippo's jaws are hinged way back in its skull. They can open about 150° (nearly half a circle), which is far wider than a human can.

TEETH
The huge teeth are like tusks and are used in fights between male hippos. For feeding, they use their rubbery lips, not their teeth, to rip up grass.

SKIN
Hippos cannot sweat to keep cool, but their skin produces a mucus that turns reddish brown in the air, and acts like a sunblock to protect them.

HEAD
The eyes, nostrils, and ears are high up on top of the head so the hippo can still see, breathe, and hear even when it is almost totally under the water.

The ancient Greeks called the hippopotamus "river horse," and it truly is a water animal. It can hold its breath underwater for five minutes, and is so huge it can walk along the bottom of rivers and lakes, although it is a good swimmer. Hippos spend most of their day in the water to keep cool, and come ashore at night to feed on grass for around six hours. They will walk up to 6 miles (9.6 km) for food, and eat 80–150 pounds (36–68 kg) a night, which is a relatively small amount for such a huge creature.

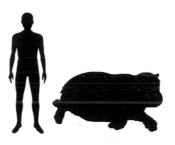

HOW BIG IS IT?

AT A GLANCE

Lifespan:	40 years
Weight:	5,000–8,000 pounds (2,270–3,600 kg)
Length:	9–14 feet (280–420 cm)
Tail Length:	20 inches (50 cm)

World Habitat
Hippos are found across the center and south of Africa.

Endangered Status

 Least Concern

DID YOU KNOW?

- Baby hippos (called calves) are born underwater and can close their ears and nostrils to drink their mother's milk underwater, too. They weigh nearly 100 pounds (45 kg) at birth and can swim as soon as they are born.

- Hippos have no real natural predators, although crocodiles, lions, leopards, wild dogs, and hyenas can attack a young or injured hippo.

- Their tusks are actually canine teeth, and can grow to be more than 1 foot (30 cm) long.

- Hippos are the third-largest land animal, after the elephant and the rhinoceros.

- A hippopotamus can run up to 19 mph (30 kph) over short distances. That's faster than an adult human can run.

Low   High

LEVEL OF THREAT TO HUMANS?

They might eat only grass, but you don't want to get close to an angry hippopotamus. They are considered the most dangerous mammal in Africa. Male hippos will fight for a mate or to protect their territory. At first they "yawn" as a threat, and make loud bellowing noises. If it comes to a fight, they thrash at each other with their strong teeth, drawing blood and sometimes fighting to the death.

KAKAPO

The kakapo's name means "night parrot" and it is a truly unusual bird. Not only is it nocturnal, it is also flightless, vegetarian, the heaviest of all parrots, and one of the longest-living birds on the planet. As it evolved, it lost the power of flight and its best form of defense now is to freeze and hope it doesn't get noticed. That was a good strategy when there were no predators, but once humans brought predatory mammals to New Zealand, the kakapo was in serious trouble.

HOW BIG IS IT?

FACE
The kakapo looks as much like an owl as a parrot, with a disk of hairlike feathers for a face. It has whiskers around its beak.

COLOR
Its mossy green feathers provide excellent camouflage in the trees, but the color doesn't help to hide it when it is on the ground.

BODY
It has a fat, round body and seems to waddle when it walks around, but its strong legs are powerful enough to enable the bird to climb trees and walk for miles.

SMELL
Kakapos are famous for their "musky" scent, which smells a little like flowers. Unfortunately, this smell attracts all sorts of predators from great distances.

AT A GLANCE

Lifespan:	60–90 years
Weight:	8.8 pounds (4 kg)
Length:	24 inches (60 cm)
Wingspan:	34 inches (87 cm)

World Habitat
The kakapo used to be widespread in New Zealand but now lives only on Codfish and Anchor Islands.

Endangered Status   Critically Endangered

DID YOU KNOW?

● Kakapos are so seriously threatened that in 1989 the only remaining ones (around 40 of them) were taken to two protected islands to be looked after. In April 2010 their numbers had risen to 125, and each bird has been given an individual name.

● The bird makes a screeching, squawking noise like other parrots, but also has sounds like a braying donkey, a squealing pig, a grunting warthog, and a booming bittern.

● It has been described as a "Dr. Seuss kind of bird" that can "hop like a sparrow and growl like a dog."

● To find a mate, the kakapo walks to the top of a hill, digs a bowl-shaped hollow called a "lek," and makes a loud booming noise that can be heard for miles around.

Low   High
LEVEL OF THREAT TO HUMANS?

The kakapo roosts in hollow trunks, under bushes, or in fallen trees. Using its long, sharp claws and strong legs, it can climb to find food or to sleep during the day. Once it is in a tree, it can walk around safely, but it has problems getting down. Often, it will just jump off a low branch, and use its wings to break its fall as it hits the ground with a bump.

KIWI

The kiwi is well known as the national bird of New Zealand, but it lives such a secretive life that not many people have seen one in the wild. Kiwis hide away in the daytime to sleep in thick vegetation, hollow logs, tree roots, or in a burrow dug by the male. When it sleeps, a kiwi tucks its head under its tiny wing. They look cute, but have sharp claws that they use to attack rivals and defend themselves. They can move really fast, and can outrun a human if they need to.

HOW BIG IS IT?

FEATHERS
A kiwi is covered in coarse fluff, which is more like fur than feathers. They are brown, with some patterns on their body.

BODY
A fat, rounded body and hunched back give the kiwi a peculiar, but easily recognizable, shape.

BEAK
Nostrils on the very tip of the long, curved beak give the kiwi an excellent sense of smell and help the bird find food hidden in the ground.

WINGS
Kiwis have no real "wingspan" because each wing is only a tiny stump measuring around 2 inches (5 cm). Their wings have grown smaller as they evolved to become flightless.

AT A GLANCE

Lifespan:	17 years
Weight:	2–8.5 pounds (0.9–3.9kg)
Length:	13.5–26 inches (34–65 cm)
Wingspan:	2 inches (5 cm)

World Habitat
Different species of kiwi live on different parts of both islands of New Zealand.

Endangered Status

Endangered

DID YOU KNOW?

- The kiwi has no tail.

- The eggs are larger (for the size of the female) than any other bird's egg. Once the mother has laid one or two eggs in the nest, she hands over to the male, who sits there until the babies hatch. He doesn't leave to eat, and can lose one-third of his body weight.

- A kiwi egg has more yolk than other birds' eggs, so the adults do not feed the baby but leave it to eat the yolk stuck to its feathers. After 6–10 days, the baby bird has to find its own food, making it very vulnerable to predators.

- Kiwis are under threat from mammals brought to New Zealand, including rats and stoats.

Low   High
LEVEL OF THREAT TO HUMANS?

A kiwi has poor eyesight, but uses its specialized beak to hunt for food such as worms, grubs, and insects. It walks along with its beak on the ground, tapping for food and sniffing with the peculiar nostrils on the very end of the bill. If it smells a buried snack, such as a grub, it can bury its beak up to 6 inches (15 cm) to grab it.

TEETH
A naked mole rat's huge front teeth stick out of its mouth, and its lips close behind them. This enables it to dig without swallowing any dirt.

EYES
Its eyes have become tiny and almost useless because it hardly needs them underground. A naked mole rat can only tell the difference between daylight and darkness.

SKIN
It isn't actually naked, but is almost hairless, and its pinky-gray wrinkled skin makes its tube-shaped body look like a wiener. It does have a few whiskers on its face for sensing things.

FEET
Thick claws and strong legs help the naked mole rat with its digging, and hairs between its toes act like a broom to sweep away the soil.

Naked mole rats are unlike most mammals. It is easy for them to keep warm underground in the desert, so they have hardly any fur. They live more like social insects (such as bees or ants) than like mammals, with a dominant female called a queen, who gives birth to all the babies in a colony. This queen cleverly controls all the other females with a special chemical that stops them from becoming pregnant. The colony is served by workers, which dig tunnels and find underground roots and tubers to eat, and soldiers, which grow larger and protect the burrow from intruders.

HOW BIG IS IT?

AT A GLANCE

Lifespan:	5 years
Weight:	1–3 ounces (28–85g)
Length:	4 inches (10 cm)
Tail Length:	1.5 inches (3.8 cm)

World Habitat
Naked mole rats live in the far eastern tip of Africa, in the dry areas of Ethiopia, Kenya, and Somalia.

Endangered Status   Least Concern

DID YOU KNOW?

• The queen can have more than 20 pups in a litter. Other naked mole rats in her colony help her to look after them.

• A naked mole rat can move its front teeth separately, to use them like chopsticks!

• Members of the same colony roll around in their toilet chamber so that they all smell the same. If a strange naked mole rat appears, the others can sniff it out unless it manages to mix with them for long enough to become "camouflaged."

• Their burrow keeps them safe from nearly all predators. Occasionally, a snake may slither down one of the holes, but the soldiers gang up to scare it away, or attack it using their large teeth.

Low   High
LEVEL OF THREAT TO HUMANS?

The worker mole rats dig in teams to make tunnels around a central chamber. These tunnels can reach 130 feet (40 m) in each direction and may be 20 inches (50 cm) underground. Around 80 naked mole rats live together in a colony in one burrow, and they dig new tunnels all the time to look for food. One worker digs ahead, and is followed by more workers who kick the loose soil back toward the surface. Here, one worker pushes all of the soil out of the exit to clear the tunnel.

NINE-BANDED ARMADILLO

NOSE
The long snout is used to sniff out food as the armadillo hunts in the darkness of night. It has excellent hearing to pick up the sounds of moving grubs.

SHELL
The "shell" is made up of bony plates and horny skin to protect the animal from predators. Eight, nine, or ten flexible bands in the middle help it move easily.

CLAWS
A nine-banded armadillo has long, sharp claws for digging for ants and other insects to eat.

SIZE
This species is about the size of a large cat, and it can jump 3–4 feet (0.9–1.2 m) straight up into the air!

These amazing animals are reversing the common trend today and actually growing in numbers and moving to more new places. They love to burrow, and dig underground dens to live in. Its body armor weighs around one-sixth of its total body weight, but is not flexible enough to allow it to roll into a ball like some armadillos. It can hunch down to the ground, though, to protect itself as much as possible. It leaps up high if it is frightened, but this makes it a hazard for drivers and puts the armadillo in danger of being killed in road accidents.

HOW BIG IS IT?

AT A GLANCE

Lifespan:	8–12 years
Adult Weight:	5½–14 pounds (2.5–6.5 kg)
Adult Length:	14–22 inches (35–57 cm)
Tail Length:	9½–18 inches (24–45 cm)

World Habitat
This armadillo is found in the southern United States, Mexico, Argentina, and Uruguay.

Endangered Status — Least Concern

DID YOU KNOW?

• This species of armadillo always has four identical babies (quadruplets) of the same sex. When they are born, their shell is soft, like leather, and grows hard only when they reach adult size.

• The nine-banded armadillo is the state animal of Texas.

• It walks slowly—only around one-third of a mile per hour (0.5 kph)—nosing around in the undergrowth, unless it is in danger, when it can run much faster.

• The three-banded armadillo can roll itself completely into a ball with its head and tail tucked inside.

• Scientists have found a species of armadillo, now extinct, that grew as big as a family car. Its armor had no hinges or bands but was a single piece, shaped like an igloo.

Low   High
LEVEL OF THREAT TO HUMANS?

This animal loves to live near water, and has amazing ways to cross streams and creeks. For narrow stretches, it sinks in the water because of its heavy shell, and simply walks across along the bottom. It can hold its breath for around six minutes. To cross wider rivers, it swallows air to fill its stomach to twice the usual size to help it float, and then swims across.

MORAY EEL

BODY
The eel's long, slender body is designed to wriggle into small gaps in the rocks and reefs, where they hide and wait for a meal to swim by.

EYES
Morays have rather poor eyesight but use their keen sense of smell to help them hunt at night.

TEETH
The scary lineup of teeth at the front are used for tearing flesh, and the moray has a second set of teeth farther back, in their throat, for dragging food into their body.

FINS
Moray eels do not have side fins, which makes them look quite snakelike, but they have a long dorsal fin running all the way down their back.

Many divers have come face to face with this underwater creature—and it's a scary sight! Moray eels hide in holes, waiting for food to pass by, such as a tasty fish, mollusk, or crustacean. Then they strike out at lightning speed and grab their prey. Their fearsome appearance is misleading. They have small gills and so have to constantly open and close their mouth to help them breathe, which makes them look more aggressive to humans than they really are. A moray will attack a diver only if it is disturbed or feels threatened.

HOW BIG IS IT?

AT A GLANCE

Lifespan:	30 years or more
Weight:	88 pounds (40 kg)
Length:	Up to 15 feet (4.5 m)

World Habitat
Moray eels like warm (tropical or temperate) shallow waters, especially around coral reefs.

Endangered Status

 Least Concern

DID YOU KNOW?

- There are more than 100 species of moray eel, in many colors and sizes. The largest is the giant moray, which can weigh more than 60 pounds (27 kg). The slender giant moray is longer but weighs less.

- It is said that King Henry I of England died after dining on a moray eel. They are not fit for humans to eat because they contain toxins passed on from their own food.

- Green moray eels actually have blue skin, but this is covered in a yellow slimy coating that makes them look green. Most morays have slime to protect them as they wriggle past sharp rocks.

- Morays really cannot see well and it's thought that injuries to divers are mostly the eel thinking the diver's finger is a food item. They can bite a person's finger right off!

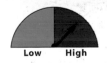

Low   High

LEVEL OF THREAT TO HUMANS?

Moray eels are often infected with parasites and worms. Some shrimps and small fish, called wrasse, love to eat these nasties, and so the morays and wrasse have formed a friendship. The wrasse keeps the eel clean and, in return, the moray doesn't eat the wrasse! The fish even swim safely in and out of the eel's mouth to clean it.

ANGEL SHARK

WINGS
The long, wide fins on the sides of the shark look like an angel's wings and so give the shark its name. It also looks like a monk's hood so is sometimes called the monkfish.

TEETH
Hidden beneath its body, at the very tip of the snout, is a mouth full of sharp triangular teeth. The angel shark has a very nasty bite.

BARBELS
The whiskery antennae by the shark's mouth are barbels. These are used to smell for prey by detecting chemicals in the water.

BODY SHAPE
The angel shark looks more like a ray or a skate than a shark, but its fins are not attached to its head like the fins of a ray.

In the daytime, the angel shark lurks on the ocean bed, buried in the sand with just its eyes showing. (This may be why the angel shark is also known as the sand devil.) It might stay in that position for days, waiting for its next victim to pass by. Angel sharks eat all sorts of fish and shellfish, including halibut, flounder, squid, and clams. They use their barbels to sense prey, but also rely heavily on sight. To hunt for food at night, they track the bioluminescent (glow-in-the-dark) plankton that trail behind the fish.

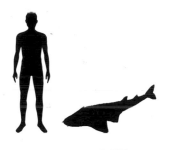

HOW BIG IS IT?

AT A GLANCE

Lifespan:	About 10 years
Weight:	60 pounds (27 kg)
Length:	6.5 feet (200 cm)

World Habitat
They can be found in the southwestern Indian Ocean, the eastern and western Pacific Ocean, and the eastern and western Atlantic Ocean.

Endangered Status — Near Threatened

DID YOU KNOW?

• Many sharks need to keep swimming to pull water over their gills in order to breathe. The angel shark can stay still because it has spiracles and muscles to pull water across as it needs.

• An angel shark mother keeps her eggs inside her body until they hatch, then mini-sharks pop out, each less than 1 foot (30 cm) long.

• Pliny the Elder of ancient Rome was a writer who also studied nature. In his book about animals, he advised that angel shark skin was good for cleaning the house and for clearing up acne.

• The angel shark is considered to be very tasty, and overfishing drastically reduced its numbers toward the end of the twentieth century. Fishing is now strictly regulated to help bring the numbers up again.

Low High
LEVEL OF THREAT TO HUMANS?

Angel sharks will bite a diver if they are provoked, but generally they limit their attacks to fish and shellfish. They push their top half off the seabed at lightning speed and can catch a passing fish in one-tenth of a second. Their tail is a different design to most sharks. Instead of having the bigger fin on top, angel sharks have it at the bottom to help push off the ocean floor.

TEETH
A wolf has long fangs at the front for stabbing into flesh, and strong teeth toward the back of its mouth for slashing and tearing at the flesh of its prey.

NOSE
The long muzzle contains sensitive smelling organs. These help the wolves track down prey by following its scent.

CLAWS
A wolf's only real weapon is its teeth because its claws are too blunt to use in the hunt. They are long and nonretractable, and used to help them run and grip.

SIZE
The gray wolf is the biggest wild dog in the world. It grows to more than 3 feet (nearly 1 m) tall at the shoulder—nearly twice the size of a domestic German Shepherd.

The mighty gray wolf, sometimes called the timber wolf, is well known for its stamina and the way it tracks its prey for miles. Although it is big, it hunts animals that are even bigger, and it needs to work in a group to be able to make the kill. A pack of wolves might follow a group of large animals for days, watching the herd to find one animal that seems old or sick. The wolves single out the weaker animal and follow it, snapping at its heels.

HOW BIG IS IT?

AT A GLANCE

Lifespan:	Up to 17 years
Weight:	40–176 pounds (18–80 kg)
Length:	3.25–5 feet (1–1.5 m)
Tail Length:	Up to 1.75 feet (50 cm)

World Habitat
Packs of wolves live and hunt in many northern territories across North America, Greenland, Europe, and Asia.

Endangered Status   Least Concern

DID YOU KNOW?

- Wolves hunt animals as much as ten times bigger than themselves, including moose, caribou, and bison.

- A young wolf is called a pup or cub. The female has 4–7 pups, which are fed on scraps of food that the other wolves in the pack eat and then regurgitate.

- Each pack has a dominant male and female. The female of this couple is the only one to have pups, and the dominant couple get the first chance to eat when the pack has made a kill.

- The gray wolf was once the world's most widespread carnivore but has been hunted out of many of its homelands. Humans are frightened by these howling night creatures and their fierce behavior—killing livestock and (in myths) preying on humans.

Low   High

LEVEL OF THREAT TO HUMANS?

Wolves live in packs and howl to communicate. A howl might be a call to rival packs to keep them off their territory and avoid fighting. Sometimes, very young and old wolves stay behind from the hunt, and the howl might let them know that the catch was made and food is there for them. A wolf's howl can be heard from as far away as 10 miles (16 km).

JAGUAR

EYES
A big cat's eyes point forward and not to the side, to give it good vision and the ability to judge distance accurately.

EARS
A jaguar has smallish, rounded ears, which help it hear the rustle of prey in the darkness, so it can creep up silently and without being seen. Jaguars also use their sensitive whiskers to feel their way through the jungle at night.

CLAWS
The curved claws point backward to help keep hold of its prey. They can be retracted (pulled inward) to stop them from getting blunt.

BODY
A jaguar is squat and strong, with powerful shoulders, a large, broad head, and extremely muscular legs.

The jaguar is very similar to the leopard but bigger. It lives near the Amazon and northward into Mexico. Its name comes from the Native American and means "he who kills with one leap." A jaguar will ambush prey from a hiding place in a tree or the undergrowth, and kill it with a single bite or swipe of their large paw. They eat capybaras, deer, tapirs, and peccaries. They love to swim, and will also catch turtles, fish, and caimans. A jaguar's teeth can bite straight through a turtle shell.

HOW BIG IS IT?

AT A GLANCE

Lifespan:	11 years
Weight:	80–350 pounds (36–160 kg)
Length:	8 feet (2.4 m)
Height:	28 inches (70 cm)

World Habitat
Jaguars love dense forests with water nearby, but live in woodland and grasslands in several parts of the Americas.

Endangered Status — Near Threatened

DID YOU KNOW?

• The jaguar is the world's third-largest cat, after the tiger and lion. It is the only "big cat" in the New World. Pumas may grow as large but do not count as big cats because they cannot roar.

• The jaguar often kills its prey with a single bite down between the ears, through the skull and straight into the brain. That takes an extremely powerful set of jaws.

• A mother jaguar brings up her cubs without the father because males are likely to kill the cubs. She has 1–4 cubs, but usually two, and they weigh around 1½ pounds (680 g) at birth.

• Jaguars were important in the belief system of ancient peoples native to the Americas. The Mayan jaguar gods were associated with caves and the night, just like the animals themselves.

Low   High

LEVEL OF THREAT TO HUMANS?

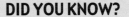 A jaguar's camouflage works so well that researchers have sometimes been standing just feet away from an animal they know is there, unable to see it unless it moves. Jaguars sleep during the day, sometimes curled in a tree with a telltale tail hanging down. They hunt as dusk falls. Each jaguar stays in its own territory, which it marks by leaving scent and scratching trees to warn away others.

LEOPARD

PAWS

A big cat has hairless pads on its feet, which are surrounded by fur to help it stalk silently. The cat can retract (pull) its claws into its toes to protect them and keep them sharp and also reduce the noise when it walks.

SENSES

The leopard has a fantastic sense of smell, hearing, and eyesight. It uses its sensitive whiskers to help it feel its way around when it hunts in the dark at night.

CLAWS

A leopard's claws are curved and super-sharp, both for catching prey and climbing trees. It can climb down a tree head-first.

HEAD

Its large head contains powerful jaws that the leopard uses to kill and pull apart its prey.

Leopards and jaguars are similar but live in different parts of the world. The leopard is smaller and not as stocky. Both have spotted markings to camouflage them in the sunlight that filters through the trees where they make their home. Leopards hunt at night, stalking large mammals such as deer, pigs, antelopes, and baboons, and can run more than 30 mph (48 kph) to catch a meal. They bite down hard on the neck or throat, and carry the dead animal up a tree to eat in peace.

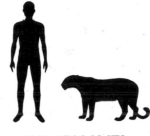

HOW BIG IS IT?

DID YOU KNOW?

• Leopards love to swim and sometimes enter the water to find food such as crabs and fish. Their jaws and teeth are strong enough to crunch through a crab's shell in no time.

• A leopard's markings are not only on its fur but on its skin, too. Some leopards (and jaguars) have black spots on a black background. These cats are nicknamed "black panthers" but that isn't a scientific name.

• A leopard was seen dragging a young giraffe into the undergrowth to hide it. The giraffe weighed 220 pounds (100 kg)—possibly more than two times the weight of the leopard.

• Leopards have to share their homelands with more humans and sometimes live near big cities. They will attack pets, livestock, and people if starving or threatened.

Low   High
LEVEL OF THREAT TO HUMANS?

Leopards are incredibly athletic, being strong, fast, and able to jump and swim well. They can leap 20 feet (6 m) forward in one bound, and jump 10 feet (3 m) straight up in the air. A leopard can carry a dead animal to heights of 50 feet (15 m) in the trees to keep it away from other predators such as lions, jackals, and hyenas. The leopard holds the animal in its teeth to climb.

HONEY BADGER

CLAWS
A honey badger needs to dig, and so nature has given it a fearsome set of claws that grow to 1.5 inches (4 cm) long.

EARS
This animal's ears have no external flaps, but the honey badger can hold the holes closed while it digs, in order to keep out the dirt.

COLOR
It is no coincidence that the honey badger shares its coloring with the skunk. Such markings are nature's warning that the animal gives off a strong stink to protect itself.

SKIN
The honey badger's skin is tough, but has the bonus of fitting loosely so that it can swing around to attack an animal holding the honey badger by the neck.

Labeled "the meanest animal in the world" and also "the most fearless" (according to *The Guinness Book of Records*), the honey badger is also known as the ratel. It is easily recognized by its black and white markings. Its nickname comes from its love of honey, and it will climb trees to get to a bees' nest. It has a strange friendship with the honeyguide bird, which leads the animal to a bees' nest and shares the meal once the honey badger has broken it open. Honey badgers eat almost anything, including small mammals, scorpions, porcupines, snakes, and insects.

HOW BIG IS IT?

AT A GLANCE

Lifespan:	Up to 8 years
Weight:	22 pounds (10 kg)
Length:	30–40 inches (0.8–1 m)
Tail:	12 inches (30 cm)

World Habitat
The honey badger adapts to many habitats, from desert to rainforest, and lives across Africa and parts of Asia.

Endangered Status   Least Concern

DID YOU KNOW?

• A *National Geographic* documentary filmed a ratel fighting a puff adder and seemingly dying from a venomous bite. However, after two hours the ratel woke up! It had only been paralyzed and had survived the attack.

• In cold weather, with no humans around, ratels hunt in the daytime, but in the hottest months, or if people live nearby, they are nocturnal.

• Ratels are clever enough to use tools. They have been seen rolling logs to stand on in order to reach food high above them.

• Honey badgers are preyed on by leopards and lions, but will readily attack them and chase them off. This creature fights so fiercely it even has an armored vehicle named after it in the South African Defense Force.

Low   High
LEVEL OF THREAT TO HUMANS?

◁ A honey badger has thick skin to protect it from stings and bites. It possibly builds up an immunity to venom from small stings and bites from scorpions, snakes, and bees. A mother honey badger stops her babies from tackling venomous snakes until they are skilled enough to take one on. The adult grabs a snake in its jaws, holding it safely behind the head so it won't get bitten, and can eat a snake 5 feet (1.5 m) long in 15 minutes!

SCREECH OWL

The screech owl is a nickname for the barn owl, but there are also 21 species of actual screech owls that live only in the Americas, and which are not closely related to the barn owl. They are small owls and great fliers, swooping down in a dive to catch rats, squirrels, shrews, moles, chipmunks, insects, and small birds such as grouse and quail. Smaller food is eaten all at once, but anything larger is taken back to the safety of the trees to tear apart and eat.

HOW BIG IS IT?

COLOR
A screech owl will often have a mottled brown or gray coloring on its top side, with a paler underside, to help it blend in with the bark of trees.

CLAWS
They have extremely sharp, curved claws to grasp their prey and carry it in flight, and to hold it while they eat.

BEAK
The screech owl's beak is curved and used to tear prey into pieces that are small enough to swallow.

DIFFERENCES
Two of the most common species of screech owl look nearly the same. However, the western screech owl has a gray-black beak and the eastern screech owl has as beak that is gray-green.

AT A GLANCE

Lifespan:	Up to 7 years
Weight:	Up to 7 ounces (200 g)
Length:	8–9 inches (20–23 cm)
Wingspan:	22 inches (56 cm)

World Habitat
Two of the most common screech owls are the western and eastern, which occupy much of North America.

Endangered Status   Least Concern

DID YOU KNOW?

• Screech owls make different noises for different things. Their piercing territorial cry sounds like a woman crying out in pain. Different calls are used by different species.

• The western screech owl hides from predators by pulling itself into a longer, thinner shape to pretend to be a tree limb.

• Screech owls choose a mate and stick together for life. If one gets killed, the other might take on a new mate. They have 4–8 eggs and the mother sits on them until they hatch. Usually only one chick survives.

• They hunt after dusk, mostly in the first few hours of darkness, but sometimes until dawn. The owl listens for prey with its superb hearing, and dives in for the kill.

Low   High
LEVEL OF THREAT TO HUMANS?

A male screech owl makes a nest in the hollow of a tree, or in the abandoned nest of another bird, and looks for a mate to share his nest. Their name comes from their eerie, wailing call, which is often heard at night in forests and backyards. The call is quite easy to copy, and humans who imitate the "screech" often hear a reply from an actual screech owl!

BODY
A hyena has a distinctive shape, with longer front legs than back legs, which make its body slope downward toward the back.

MANE
All hyenas have a kind of mane running from their neck down their back. The spotted hyena's is reversed, as the hairs slope forward instead of backward.

JAWS
The spotted hyena has the most powerful jaws of any mammal of this size. They can crush bone and chew easily through animal skin.

DIGESTION
Unlike many meat-eaters, spotted hyenas can digest skin and bones. They get lots of their nutrition from bone marrow. Parts of their prey that they cannot digest, such as hooves and hair, are regurgitated as pellets.

Spotted hyenas live and hunt in packs, and can easily tackle animals larger than themselves. A clan of hyenas contains from five to 50 animals, depending on how much food there is where they live. A large clan can bring down a zebra, wildebeest, or buffalo, or can scare away lions— even while they are feeding— and scavenge their meal. They hunt at night and can easily be heard in the darkness when they make their characteristic "laugh," which sounds like wild cackling. Hyenas can run fast, and cover long distances during a hunt.

HOW BIG IS IT?

AT A GLANCE

Lifespan:	12 years
Weight:	150 pounds (70 kg)
Length:	4.5 feet (1.3 m)
Tail Length:	10 inches (25 cm)

World Habitat
Hyenas live across Africa, in many habitats, from savanna and woodlands to mountains and the edge of deserts.

Endangered Status — Least Concern

DID YOU KNOW?

- There are three species of hyena: spotted, brown, and striped. The spotted hyena is the biggest and also the fiercest hunter. Striped and brown hyena scavenge more often than they hunt.

- A hyena's mane stands on end when it is excited.

- A spotted hyena can run at 30 mph (48 kph) for up to 2 miles (3.25 km), and can also swim well.

- Hyenas look similar to dogs, but are scientifically more closely related to cats.

- They have many calls as well as their famous "laugh." They whoop, groan, squeal, snarl, and growl. Some of the noises they make are too quiet for humans to hear.

Low High

LEVEL OF THREAT TO HUMANS?

More and more frequently, the territory of humans and hyenas overlaps, and hyenas are often blamed for raids on farm livestock. They are sometimes also accused of human killings, and are hunted to keep them away from homes and villages. However, the Maasai people of Kenya and Tanzania make use of the hyena's habits and leave their dead to be eaten by hyenas instead of burying them.

TASMANIAN DEVIL

TAIL
A Tasmanian devil's tail stores fat, so you can tell if the animal is well fed by how swollen or shrunken its tail looks.

POUCH
This creature is a marsupial, meaning that the female has a pouch where its tiny newborn babies grow bigger. The female Tasmanian devil's pouch opens backward to keep out dirt when she digs.

EARS
Its ears are usually a pale pink color but they turn red when the animal gets angry.

NOSE
The animal has a great sense of smell, which it uses to find food, especially the bodies of dead animals, where groups of Tasmanian devils gather to eat.

These creatures were named by travelers who saw them reacting to an attack with a display of growling, snarling, screaming, and teeth-baring. If you have seen Taz, the cartoon character that is a Tasmanian devil, you will know what its reputation is, and it's not too greatly exaggerated. They are ferocious animals that put up a real fight and have sharp teeth and a very strong bite. They rest in a hollow log or a burrow during the daytime, and come out at night to eat. Their long whiskers help them to find their way in the darkness.

HOW BIG IS IT?

AT A GLANCE

Lifespan:	8 years
Weight:	9–26 pounds (4–12 kg)
Length:	20–31 inches (51–79 cm)
Tail Length:	9–12 inches (23–30 cm)

World Habitat
These creatures live only on the island of Tasmania, off the coast of Australia. They used to live all over the mainland.

Endangered Status   Endangered

DID YOU KNOW?

• Unfortunately, Tasmanian devil numbers have dropped recently because of an illness called Devil Facial Tumor Disease (DFTD), which results in such bad swelling around the mouth that the animals starve to death.

• The babies are the size of a grain of rice when they are born. They drag themselves to their mother's pouch and find a nipple to drink milk.

• A Tasmanian devil has several forms of defense. It may yawn to show its teeth (or pretend it is not threatened by its attacker), raise its tail, make its characteristic screeching howl, or let off a strong smell like a skunk.

• A single devil can eat as much as 40 percent of its own body weight in food in just half an hour.

Low   High
LEVEL OF THREAT TO HUMANS?

Tasmanian devils live alone but crowd together to eat from the same carcass, pushing and snarling to get the best eating place. They prefer meat from an animal that is already dead, and are wholly carnivorous. They will also kill for food, delivering a bite to the neck to finish off small prey. They attack snakes, lizards, rodents, and birds, and eat the whole thing—skin, bones, meat, and even fur and feathers.

BANDICOOT

LEGS
A bandicoot hops around on its hind legs like a small version of a kangaroo. Some species stamp on their food before eating it.

POUCH
The mother's pouch faces backward to protect the babies inside it from dirt that gets thrown around when she is digging a burrow.

CLAWS
The front claws are strong for digging. The back claws are also powerful but have two toes fused into one, the same way a kangaroo's foot has.

NOSE
Bandicoots have a long, slim nose that tapers to a slender end, which they use for rooting in dirt and digging into cracks for food.

The bandicoot should be a welcome yard visitor because it eats pests such as insects and grubs. Bandicoots forage for food at night, and leave distinctive (often unwanted) snout-shaped holes in people's lawns. They have few native predators but their numbers are in decline because of vehicle accidents and because introduced animals such as pet cats, dogs, and wild foxes threaten them. Bandicoots are marsupials, like koalas, opossums, and Tasmanian devils, so their babies grow larger in their mother's pouch. Many bandicoots are about the size of a rabbit.

HOW BIG IS IT?

AT A GLANCE

Lifespan:	3–7 years
Weight:	Up to 3 pounds (1.4 kg)
Length:	Up to 14 inches (36 cm)
Tail Length:	The same as the body length

World Habitat
The longnosed bandicoot is found mainly in forests to the east of Australia , from Cooktown to Victoria.

Endangered Status — Least Concern

DID YOU KNOW?

• Its name comes from the Telugu Indian word "bandi," meaning "pig." The name was originally used for the Indian animal, the bandicoot rat, which is not related to the Australian bandicoots.

• Bandicoots do, however, sound like a pig when foraging. They snuffle while they look for food and grunt when they find it.

• Many females can have babies every seven weeks. She usually has two or three babies in each litter. Not all the babies survive once they leave the pouch because they make easy pickings for birds of prey, dingos, and snakes.

• The bandicoot has an excellent sense of smell and hearing, so it can hunt in the dark. It listens and sniffs for grubs and beetles so that it knows exactly where to dig.

Low   High

LEVEL OF THREAT TO HUMANS?

Male bandicoots have their own territory, which they mark with scent and defend from other males. The two male bandicoots will stand on their back legs and fight with their claws. They sometimes dance or wind around each other and can throw each other around like judo fighters. The combat might be done in silence or with barking and snorting. They can really hurt each other.

BARN OWL

FACE
Distinctive and easy to recognize, the barn owl's face is heart-shaped and pale.

EYES
The owl's eyes, which are dark circles in its white face, can spot tiny movements on the ground.

EARS
An owl's ears are just openings in the side of the head, behind and below the eyes, and covered by feathers.

BEAK
The owl carries its prey back to its roost in its sharp, hooked beak.

TALONS
Strong, feathered legs end in powerful feet and sharp claws. The owl adjusts them to the right size and shape during flight to hook up its prey instantly.

FEATHERS
Very soft feathers muffle the flapping of the wings in flight, enabling the owl to fly almost silently.

The barn owl is sometimes called the screech owl, because it makes a spooky, shrieking cry instead of the expected hoot. Like other owls, it doesn't make a nest, but lays its eggs in hollow trees or small spaces in buildings, such as the barns that give the bird its name. Its heart-shaped face helps to channel tiny sounds so that it can hear exceptionally well. Its eyes face forward, enabling it to judge distances by sight, but its eyeballs do not move around as much as those of a mammal. Instead, it can turn its head nearly a full circle to let it see in all directions.

HOW BIG IS IT?

AT A GLANCE

Lifespan:	Nearly 18 years
Weight:	8–16 ounces (225–450 g)
Length:	11–15 inches (30–40 cm)
Wingspan:	33 inches (85 cm)

World Habitat
Barn owls are one of the world's most widespread birds. They live on every continent except Antarctica.

Endangered Status   Least Concern

DID YOU KNOW?

- An owl has a third eyelid, which flicks across its eyeball to clean it.

- Barn owls are active at night, but often hunt at dawn and dusk, when they can use their acute eyesight as well as their sharp hearing.

- The eggs are laid over a few days, so a baby owl may be a week younger than its brother or sister.

- Barn owls love to hunt near highways, where food is plentiful in the grass at the roadside. Unfortunately, they fly 7–8 feet (2.1–2.4 m) above the ground, and are often hit by traffic.

- Although barn owls are not endangered, their numbers are dropping because of loss of habitat, changes in farming (including using harmful pesticides), and many road deaths.

Low   High
LEVEL OF THREAT TO HUMANS?

Small mammals, such as voles and rats, are the favorite food of a barn owl, though it will eat birds and frogs. Superb hearing lets it pinpoint rustling sounds in the undergrowth, and it swoops silently to catch prey. About six hours after its meal, the owl regurgitates the hard parts of the meal, such as bones and teeth, rolled into a pellet wrapped with fur. Barn owls cannot hunt well in rain because their feathers are not waterproof.

EYES
The two "eyes" on the beetle's back are fake, to make it look scary to predators, and as if it can see everything. Its real eyes are in a notch at the front.

THORAX
The thorax (the mid-section of an insect) has a special catch underneath that enables the click beetle to bend in half and snap back together with a "click."

SHAPE
Most click beetles are shaped like long, stretched ovals with a narrower back end than front end, much like a bullet. They come in all sizes, up to almost 2 inches (5 cm) in length.

WINGS
Click beetles are recognizable from the grooves running down the length of their hard wing covers.

This beetle could have been invented by a toymaker. If it falls, or is turned over onto its back, it plays dead and also looks just like a piece of wood. When it thinks the danger has passed, it arches its body and suddenly straightens again. This not only makes the loud click that gives the beetle its name, but shoots it up into the air so that it can turn over and land the right way up. If not, it just tries again until finds its feet and can scuttle to safety.

HOW BIG IS IT?

AT A GLANCE

Lifespan: Up to 4 years
Weight: Undetermined
Length: $^1/_2$–1$^3/_4$ inches
              (12–45 mm)

World Habitat
There are more than 9,000 species of click beetle around the world, with at least 900 in North America alone.

Endangered
Status   Least
                Concern

DID YOU KNOW?

• Click beetles can be found in all sorts of habitats, but find it hard to survive in flooded areas or deserts with no vegetation.

• It's hard for a predator to munch on a click beetle or its larvae. The larvae have a hard body, which makes them unappetizing, and they spend lots of time underground. The adult beetles often frighten off a predator with their startling "click."

• They are nocturnal, when the weather is warm enough, and diurnal (active in the daytime) if the climate is cool and they need the sunshine to warm them up.

• Some tropical species are brightly colored, like jewels. Certain species make their own light, and have glowing dots on their body like headlights or Christmas tree lights.

Low   High
LEVEL OF THREAT TO HUMANS?

Like all beetles, they start life as eggs and hatch into larvae (grubs) before pupating and becoming adults. Click beetle grubs are often called wireworms and look like hard, yellowish mealworms. They are a nuisance to farmers and gardeners because they munch their way through plants and roots and can ruin crops. Some of them are predators and eat other insect larvae.

FUR
Black under its tummy, but gray on top of its body, the badger is most famous for its white face with black stripes over its eyes.

CLAWS
The badger's 1-inch (2.5-cm) claws are useful for digging and searching for food. The badger's foot, which has five clawed toes and a wide pad, leaves behind a distinctive print.

BODY
Short legged, heavy, and squat, a badger's body is very powerful. A badger shuffles rather than runs, and rolls from side to side as it moves.

SENSES
A European badger has a good sense of smell and average hearing, but poor eyesight. However, it doesn't need to see well in the dark of night, or underground.

Badgers are related to weasels and otters, in a family called Mustelids. There are different types of badger, with the European badger being perhaps the most distinctive. These animals are secretive and hard to see, and do most things under cover of darkness. They are classed as carnivores but eat nearly anything they can find, including eggs, fruit, plants, fungi, carrion, frogs, insects, grubs, and worms. They can eat several hundred worms each night! Badgers dig with their front claws and push away the dirt with their back feet. Their eyes have a see-through layer of skin to protect them as they dig.

HOW BIG IS IT?

AT A GLANCE

Lifespan:	7–10 years
Weight:	22–35 pounds (10–16 kg)
Length:	Up to 35 inches (90 cm)
Tail Length:	Up to 8 inches (20 cm)

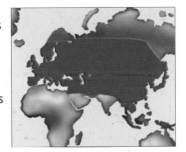

World Habitat
This type of badger lives in most parts of Europe, except the very coldest parts. It also lives across Asia into Japan.

Endangered Status   Least Concern

DID YOU KNOW?

- The American badger is related to the European badger and looks fairly similar, with black and white face markings. It eats more meat than the European badger and spends much of its time hunting.

- Wisconsin adopted the badger as its state animal in 1957.

- Setts usually have at least ten entrance holes but sometimes have as many as 100. They also have separate chambers to use as toilets.

- The German name for badger is "dachs," which gave the "dachshund" breed of dog its name because the dogs were used for chasing badgers.

Low   High
LEVEL OF THREAT TO HUMANS?

- A badger's skin is very loose, which lets it twist around if it is caught by a predator, and bite back to get away.

A badger lives in a sett, dug by itself—or by its relatives over many years. The sett has entrance holes, tunnels, and chambers where a family group live together. Some setts are known to be more than a hundred years old. The entrance is shaped like a D on its side, and is usually dug into a slope. The badgers make a nest lined with leaves, moss, and dry grass in one of the chambers, and sleep there during the day.

HEDGEHOG

SPIKES
A hedgehog has between 5,000 and 7,000 quills on its body. These hollow hairs are made spiky with keratin, which is the same substance your fingernails are made of.

NOSE
The long, flexible snout is used for finding food on the ground. It snuffles around like a pig, which explains its name, hedgehog.

BELLY
The underside, and the head and feet are covered in coarse, gray-brown fur and not spines. This means they must be drawn in for protection.

TAIL
The hedgehog has a small tail about 1 inch (2.5 cm), which it keeps tucked away. Even though it is short, the tail can be used for an extra "push" to help the hedgehog get through a small hole.

This prickly little customer is common in many parts of Europe, and found through Asia and Africa, but there are no hedgehogs native to Australia or North America. The Western European hedgehog has adapted well to life with humans nearby, and can be seen on its nightly hunting expeditions, running surprisingly fast on legs that emerge from its spiked body. Hedgehogs can reach speeds of more than 4½ mph (7 kph) and can also swim well, and climb walls, trees, and even fences. They sleep during the day, in holes or under rocks or vegetation.

HOW BIG IS IT?

DID YOU KNOW?

● Hedgehogs eat whatever they can find. They love earthworms, insects, berries, eggs, snails, frogs, mushrooms, and even carrion.

● Humans should welcome a hedgehog into their yard because they keep pests under control. They can be tempted with dog food but are best left to find their own food naturally. A single hedgehog can eat 7 ounces (200 g) of insects a night—that's a lot of bugs!

● During the winter, a hedgehog may hibernate to survive cold conditions and lack of food. Its body slows down to around 100 times less than its normal rate. This is not an actual sleeping state, and it may emerge every few days to try to find something to eat.

● Baby hedgehogs have no spines at birth but are covered with short white hairs.

Low   High
LEVEL OF THREAT TO HUMANS?

As part of its spiky defenses, the hedgehog has the ability to roll up into a tight ball with prickles pointing out on all sides. Many predators make a tentative poke at the spines with their sensitive nose or pads of their paws, and decide to leave it alone. Some desert-dwelling hedgehogs have fewer spines and so are more likely to run than roll up.

RACCOON

HANDS
A raccoon has hands, rather than paws, on its front feet, which it uses to collect and eat food. Raccoons are so skillful they can open doors and latches with their hands.

FACE
The distinctive mask of dark fur makes its small eyes seem bigger. It has a pointed snout and a keen sense of smell.

FINGERS
The skin on the fingertips of the raccoon's five long fingers is covered with lots of sensitive cells to increase their sense of touch and enable them to feel tiny differences in texture on their food.

TAIL
The dark and pale rings on the tail are among the raccoon's most distinctive features.

A raccoon's favorite place to live is not in a city, but in woodlands with water nearby. However, because of a huge increase in their numbers, raccoons have had to find new habitats. They are such adaptable animals that they have moved into urban areas and make the most of their human neighbors for food and shelter. They are well known for raiding trash cans at night. They make a den in anything suitable they can find, such as a tree hole, among rocks, under an outbuilding, or in an attic or cellar. The female has three or four babies, which leave the nest at nine weeks and are independent by six months.

HOW BIG IS IT?

AT A GLANCE

Lifespan:	Up to 16 years
Weight:	12–35 pounds (5.4–15.8 kg)
Length:	16–26 inches (40–65 cm)
Tail Length:	10–14 inches (25–35 cm)

World Habitat
The North American raccoon lives across the continent, in a range of habitats from cities to forests, marshes, and prairies.

Endangered Status   Least Concern

DID YOU KNOW?

• Raccoons have been seen "washing" their food—not to clean it, but to wet it. Scientists think this helps their sense of touch, or it may be a habit because their most common foods are caught in the water.

• A raccoon can hear a worm rustling in the undergrowth. It will grab the worm as it wriggles underground, and pull it gently so that it doesn't break in half and escape.

• Baby raccoons are often born in a tree nest and spend their first weeks high off the ground.

• In stories, raccoons are often shown as crafty or sly, possibly because they are clever enough to open containers and raid human sites. In tests, raccoons have been able to remember what to do three years after being first tested.

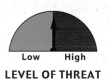

Low   High
LEVEL OF THREAT TO HUMANS?

In rural areas, raccoons fish for food, grabbing shellfish, frogs, and fish from the water. They also eat fruit, roots, nuts, eggs, insects, worms, and even birds and reptiles. Raccoons hunt mostly in the dark, so they use their sensitive fingertips to tell the difference between ripe and unripe fruit just by touch. Some northerly raccoons eat huge amounts in spring and summer to store body fat so they can sleep through the winter.

AYE-AYE

HANDS
Each hand has an extremely long, skinny middle finger, sometimes three times longer than the other fingers. All the fingers have sharp claws.

EARS
An aye-aye's ears are large and leathery. They move and twitch to pick up the tiniest sounds.

EYES
The aye-aye has large eye sockets and yellow eyes that reflect the light. This increases the amount of light falling on special cells and gives it better night vision.

FUR
The fur is dark brown or black with a few white hairs mixed in around its head and neck. Its tail is long and bushy.

Madagascar has no woodpeckers to eat the larvae of wood-boring beetles. Instead, a type of lemur, called the aye-aye, has adapted the same hunting and eating habits. The aye-aye uses its fingers to tap on trees and seek out food, just like a woodpecker pecks with its beak. These nocturnal mammals live in the treetops, and have sharp claws to help them climb through the branches. They sleep in a nest during the daytime, and use their sharp eyesight and hearing to search for food at night. As well as munching on grubs, they also eat coconuts, fruit, seeds, and fungi.

HOW BIG IS IT?

AT A GLANCE

Lifespan:	10 years
Weight:	6.6 pounds (3 kg)
Length:	16 inches (40 cm)
Tail Length:	16 in (40 cm)

World Habitat
Like all lemurs, the aye-aye lives only on the island of Madagascar, off the eastern coast of Africa.

Endangered Status   Near Threatened

DID YOU KNOW?

• The aye-aye is the world's largest nocturnal primate. Other primates include monkeys, apes, and humans.

• It was discovered in the late 1700s, but scientists first thought it was a rodent because of its long front teeth. These teeth are worn away by all the gnawing it does, but keep growing all the time.

• Madagascans are superstitious about the aye-aye and think that seeing one is a sign of bad luck. Its numbers are threatened, partly because of hunting but mostly because its habitat is being destroyed.

• The aye-aye was thought extinct in the mid-twentieth century but was seen again in 1957.

• The aye-aye can tap its fingers on a tree as rapidly as 40 times a minute.

Low   High
LEVEL OF THREAT TO HUMANS?

The aye-aye is well adapted to find food. It uses its extra-long fingers to tap on the trunk and branches of trees, and listens with its sensitive ears for hollow spaces and burrowing larvae. Its long front teeth gnaw away the wood to reveal a grub, which it skewers on its spiky long finger. Baby aye-ayes learn from their mother how to tap for food, which is a specialized skill that requires a large brain and a lot of practice.

BINTURONG

It's not hard to see why these animals are called "bear cats"—they have the face of a cat and the body of a small bear. They amble along, sometimes on the ground, but mostly in the trees, gathering fruit and leaves. They also eat carrion, fish, birds, and bugs. They can be found sunbathing or sleeping high in the trees during the day, curled up with their head under their tail. They go on the prowl for food at night.

HOW BIG IS IT?

TAIL
The bones at the end of a binturong's tail are much shorter than those near its rear end. Strong muscles enable it to wrap its tail around a tree to hold on tight.

FUR
A binturong has a long, shaggy black coat and it has been described as looking like "a yard-long black hearth rug" or a "gigantic dust mop."

SMELL
These animals have an extremely strong smell which, to a human, is most similar to the smell of fresh buttered popcorn or corn chips.

TEETH
A binturong's teeth are a mixture of sharp front teeth, for biting, and strong, flat side teeth, for chewing and grinding leaves, seeds, and fruit.

AT A GLANCE

Lifespan:	20 years in captivity
Weight:	Up to 30 pounds (14 kg)
Length:	24–38 inches (61–96 cm)
Tail Length:	Almost as long as body

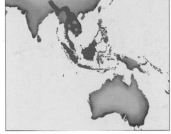

World Habitat
These creatures are found in the central Himalayas, down through Malaysia to Indonesia.

Endangered Status Vulnerable

DID YOU KNOW?

• Binturongs will not attack a human, but will defend themselves if they are threatened. They have a really strong bite, and make lots of loud noises, including growling, spitting, grunting, and hissing.

• A binturong will stand on its rear legs and puff itself up as large as it possibly can, looking more like a bear than ever, to try to frighten off attackers.

• These animals are classified as carnivores, but eat more plant matter than they do meat. They are one of only two carnivores that have a prehensile tail.

• These are the only animals known to be able to digest the hard seeds of the strangler fig, an important rainforest plant. They spread the seeds around the forest in their poop, helping to grow new trees.

Low   High
LEVEL OF THREAT TO HUMANS?

Binturongs spend most of their time in trees and have adapted extremely well to getting around in the branches. As well as using their prehensile tail for extra grip when climbing, they wrap it around a branch to anchor them while they sleep. Amazingly, the binturong can turn its ankles backward so that its claws can still grip onto the tree when it climbs down headfirst.

GREEN TREE PYTHON

HEAD
Like many tree-dwelling snakes, the green tree python's head weighs very little, so that it can strike out from the branches to catch prey.

LIPS
Special sensors on the python's lips enable it to sense heat changes, so it can tell if a mammal is passing, even in total darkness.

COLOR
As you can guess from the name, this snake is green—but some have yellow or blue markings on their body. They are still superbly camouflaged in the trees.

COILS
The snake coils itself across the branches, a bit like a bunch of unripe bananas, with its head in the middle, waiting for supper.

The green tree python is aptly named—it is bright green and spends most of its time in the trees, but it is known to hunt on the ground at night. Green tree pythons don't grow as big as some other types of python because it would be hard work moving through their treetop homes. They spend much of their time completely still, to catch their food and avoid being spotted by predators, such as the harpy eagle.

HOW BIG IS IT?

AT A GLANCE

Lifespan:	20 years
Weight:	2 pounds (1 kg)
Length:	4–7 feet (1.2–2.1 m)

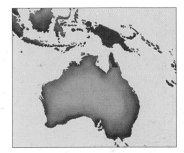

World Habitat
The green tree python lives in the rainforests of New Guinea, the world's largest island, and the north of Australia.

Endangered Status Near Threatened

DID YOU KNOW?

• While all adults are green, sometimes with different-colored markings, the babies are bright yellow, red, or brownish-red and change color as they grow older. Babies may be a completely different color from their brothers and sisters.

• A green tree python has a strong prehensile tail that helps it to hold on in the trees by winding around the branches.

• They rarely need to drink at ground level because they get moisture from droplets on leaves high in the trees.

• Green tree pythons look similar to the South American emerald tree boa, but are unrelated. Scientists call this "convergent evolution" where two species have evolved the same way to live in the same conditions, but thousands of miles apart.

Low   High
LEVEL OF THREAT TO HUMANS?

Coiled motionless in the branch of a tree, the python waits to strike. It lets its tail dangle down below its body to encourage small mammals, such as opossums and bats (and sometimes birds), to come close enough to see what it is, and then lunges at it with its mouth wide open. Its curved teeth close around its victim, which it either swallows alive or crushes in its coils first.

KOALA

Koalas like to sleep—a lot. They feed for between four and six hours, usually during the night, but the food they eat takes so long to digest that they snooze for the remaining 20 hours in a day. They have a very limited diet, and mostly eat the leaves from eucalyptus trees, which are too toxic for many other creatures to eat. A koala spends most of its time in the trees, and does not even make a nest but just wedges itself between branches to sleep. Koalas rarely drink because the leaves they eat supply enough moisture.

HOW BIG IS IT?

CLAWS
A koala's hands and feet have needle-sharp claws to help it grip onto branches and tree trunks.

BODY
The koala is a compact climbing creature, with short, muscular legs and feet that help it to stay safe high in the trees.

POUCH
The koala is a marsupial, which means that the female keeps her young safe, warm, and fed in her pouch. Babies stay with their mother for six months after they are born.

FUR
Their fur is thick and almost waterproof, and smells of eucalyptus because that is nearly all they eat.

AT A GLANCE

Lifespan:	13–18 years
Weight:	Male 26 pounds (12 kg); female 18 lbs (8 kg)
Length:	2–3 feet (60–90 cm)

World Habitat
Koalas are found in eucalyptus forests and woodlands down the eastern coast of Australia.

Endangered Status   Least Concern

DID YOU KNOW?

● When it is breeding season, the males "bellow" from the trees throughout the night. This sounds like a cross between a snore and a belch!

● Koalas in different parts of Australia like to eat different types of eucalyptus. They vary their diet sometimes by eating from trees such as the wattle, paperbark, or teatree.

● A joey eats its mother's droppings! This soft, runny poop (called "pap") helps to prepare the baby's system to digest the toxic leaves it will eat as an adult.

● Koalas sometimes climb down from their treetop home and run across to another tree. They can also leap from tree to tree. When on the ground, they have been seen licking or eating dirt to help their digestion.

Low   High
LEVEL OF THREAT TO HUMANS?

Baby koalas are known as joeys. When they are born, they measure less than 1 inch (2.5 cm) long. They crawl up their mother's underside to nestle in her pouch, where they suckle (drink milk) for six months. A young koala clings onto its mother's back as she climbs and eats. Koalas are sometimes taken by large birds of prey, but are mostly killed on the ground by domestic dogs or in car accidents.

LORIS

FEET
Each foot has four toes facing one way, and a fifth that faces the other way to allow for a tight grasp around the branches.

TEETH
The front teeth are arranged like a comb. The loris uses its teeth to clean their fur and to scrape the bark of trees to get resin.

POISON
A patch on the slow loris's elbow stores venom, which the loris sucks into its mouth, mixes around in its saliva, and then delivers in a poisonous bite.

EYES
The loris has huge eyes that face forward to help them judge distance accurately. The back of the eye reflects light to help the loris see better in the dark.

The slow loris lives up to its name, crawling through the trees at a careful pace. By day, it curls up in a ball with its head between its back legs and sleeps in the trees. At night it looks for food, moving through branches on all fours. It eats tree sap, fruit, and eggs, and live insects, slugs, snails, lizards, and birds. These may be stunned with a poisonous bite, which the loris also uses as protection against predators.

HOW BIG IS IT?

AT A GLANCE

Lifespan:	20 years
Weight:	4.5 pounds (2 kg)
Length:	10–15 inches (26–38 cm)
Tail Length:	Less than 1 inch (2.5 cm)

World Habitat
They live in tropical or swampy woodlands in Southeast Asia, from south China and Thailand to Borneo and the Philippines.

Endangered Status   Vulnerable

DID YOU KNOW?

• There is a similar creature called the slender loris, which lives only in India and Sri Lanka. It is, as you would think, skinnier than the slow loris.

• Loris mothers have one or two babies at a time. To start with, the baby clings to the fur on its mother's belly. After a few days, the mother hides it in thick leaves and wanders off to collect food.

• Superstitious beliefs and traditional medicine have put the loris at risk. Some people believe that burying a loris beneath a new road will guard against accidents, and various parts of a loris's body are used in the belief that they cure ailments.

• The slow loris is the world's only venomous primate. Primates include humans, apes, monkeys, and lemurs.

Low   High
LEVEL OF THREAT TO HUMANS?

This loris moves slowly but can act fast if it needs to do so. It will creep up on its prey stealthily and quietly, but when the loris is within reach, it quickly grabs its food before the creature can escape. The loris can hold on to a branch with its back feet so tightly that it can dangle upside down and use its front paws to grab a bite to eat.

RED-EYED TREE FROG

COLORS
The bright colors of the frog's feet, eyes, and sides are meant to startle a potential predator. A moment's hesitation about whether to eat the frog or not are all it needs to hop to safety.

TONGUE
The frog has a long, sticky tongue, which it uses to scoop up insects and then gobble them down.

LEGS
A tree frog's legs are longer than those of water-based frogs, making them better adapted for climbing than for swimming.

EYES
It is obvious where these frogs get their name. Their red eyes give the frog excellent vision, and have a third eyelid to protect the eyeball.

These frogs are a symbol of the rainforests, but are not often seen because of their nocturnal lifestyle. By day, they sleep underneath a leaf, stuck to the bottom of the foliage. They fold their legs at their sides to cover their markings and remain camouflaged with only their green back showing. At night, they hide in the leaves and ambush insects, such as crickets, moths, and flies. They use their bright colors to escape from predators.

HOW BIG IS IT?

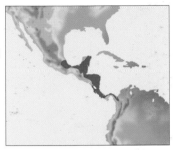
DID YOU KNOW?

● These frogs eat mostly insects, but have been known to eat anything that will fit into their mouth, even other small frogs.

● The frog's bright green color acts as camouflage, but may also help to confuse a predator. The brightness of the frog leaves a faint, ghostly image in the predator's eyes, which lingers after the frog has jumped away.

● Adult frogs are wary of snakes and birds, but the eggs are vulnerable and often get eaten by snakes and wasps. The babies inside the egg can tell what is attacking them and sometimes try to hatch early to escape.

● Frogs are amphibians and so breathe air with lungs, but the tadpoles have gills to breathe in the water until their lungs develop and their bodies grow into frog form.

Low   High
LEVEL OF THREAT TO HUMANS?

◁ Although these frogs climb better than they swim or walk, they have to gather around water to breed. The males sit on branches overhanging a pond and make clicking noises to attract a female. She lays between 20 and 60 eggs under a leaf. When these hatch into tadpoles, the tadpoles drop into the water to grow and change into baby frogs.

TARSIER

EYES
The tarsier's huge, distinctive eyes give it fantastic eyesight to enable it to hunt moving creatures at night. Each eyeball is bigger than the tarsier's brain.

FEET
The small claws sticking at right angles off the tarsier's toes are for grooming their fur. Each toe has a kind of friction pad to help with climbing.

EARS
The ears are huge and can move to pick up any tiny sounds made by potential prey.

LEGS
A tarsier's back legs are twice as long as its body and enable it to make huge leaps from tree to tree. They land feet first and then hang on with their arms.

The tarsier is one of the world's most striking creatures. Its extraordinary eyes are the biggest, in proportion to body size, of any mammal. It can even see in color, which some nocturnal creatures can't do. It is carnivorous, eating insects, baby birds, small lizards, and even snakes, and it is a fierce hunter. The creature spends nearly all of its life in the trees because it cannot walk along the ground; it has to hop to get anywhere.

HOW BIG IS IT?

AT A GLANCE

Lifespan:	12 years
Weight:	0.18–0.4 pounds (80–165 g)
Length:	3–6 inches (8–15 cm)
Tail Length:	5–11 inches (13–28 cm)

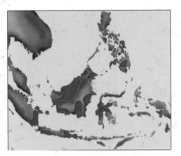

World Habitat
The tarsier lives on the islands of Indonesia, the Philippines, Malaysia, and Borneo.

Endangered Status — Least Concern

DID YOU KNOW?

● If our eyes were the same size as a tarsier's in proportion to our skull, each of our eyeballs would be as large as a grapefruit!

● Tarsiers leap around to move through the treetops. Some can jump more than 16 feet (5 m)! Their legs have very strong muscles and weigh about one-quarter of their total body weight.

● Predators include monitor lizards, birds of prey, civets, and tree snakes. Some types of tarsier gang up on a snake to frighten it away. All the members of a group will rush to the snake, lunging, biting, and making noise to scare it off.

● These animals are primates, the same as monkeys, apes, and humans, but are the only primate that does not eat any plants at all. They are related to aye-ayes and lorises.

Low   High

LEVEL OF THREAT TO HUMANS?

Although its eyes are huge and see well, they do not move in their head the way a human's eyes do. Instead, the tarsier can twist its head nearly 180° in each direction to see behind it. If it hears an insect, it swivels its head and reacts quickly enough to grab a fast-flying insect out of the air in a split second.

VIRGINIA OPOSSUM

The Virginia opossum is a marsupial, which means that it gives birth to tiny, helpless babies, about the size of a honeybee. These babies crawl into their mother's pouch to feed and grow, and then hitch a ride on her back for a while longer. Virginia opossums are the only marsupial native to North America, and the biggest ones in the New World. They like to live near humans and scavenge food from garbage at night. They eat all sorts of things, from roadkill, eggs, and grubs to nuts, fruit, and flowers.

HOW BIG IS IT?

TAIL
The hairless tail is partly prehensile (able to grasp objects). This means the opossum can use it to cling on to branches.

FUR
The Virginia opossum has pale fur on its face, and its body can be gray, red, brown, or black. It often looks scruffy because it has patches of white-tipped hairs.

POUCH
Like all marsupials, baby opossums live in the mother's pouch where they drink milk until they have grown big enough to take care of themselves.

CLAWS
Five long claws on each foot help them climb trees. They may make nests in tree holes, piles of rubble or even in sheds, chimneys, attics, and under porches.

AT A GLANCE

Lifespan:	2 years
Weight:	7–13 pounds (3–6 kg)
Length:	23–40 inches (58–100 cm) (nose to tail)

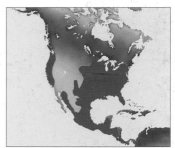

World Habitat
Virginia opossums live in Central America, Mexico, and many parts of the United States (where they are sometimes hunted as food).

Endangered Status — Least Concern

DID YOU KNOW?

• A mother will have as many as 20 babies in one litter, but only has enough nipples in her pouch to feed 13 of them. Some don't survive the crawl up to her pouch, and others starve.

• When it is "playing possum," the animal gives off a foul smelling liquid from its rear end to help keep away persistent predators.

• Their pointed snouts hide 50 tiny, sharp teeth that they bare in a snarl to try to frighten off predators. They don't like to bite, though—they just keep their mouth wide open all the time!

• Opossums adapt well to new environments, and their numbers are increasing because they benefit from human habitation rather than suffering from habitat loss. They are seen as pests in places where they destroy garden plants and raid farms or trash cans.

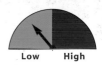

Low   High
LEVEL OF THREAT TO HUMANS?

This creature is possibly most famous for its defense strategy. When it is threatened, it rolls over and pretends to be dead. It lies on its side, staring into space with its tongue hanging out. It can stay curled up and motionless for up to six hours, in the hope that any predators lose interest and leave it alone. This faking is known as "playing possum."

INDEX